THE LABRADOR
RETRIEVER BIBLE

ASHLEY PEARSON

A Labrador is the only thing in the world that will love you more than you love yourself.

— Unknown

CONTENTS

ABOUT THE AUTHOR

Ashely Pearson is a psychologist, writer and avid dog lover. She was born and raised on the east coast of Australia in a small town called Ballina, growing up with her beloved dog named Rocky.

She has owned and looked after many dogs throughout her life, and has worked as a dog trainer over the years, doing classes and private lessons.

Accumulating a wealth of information over the last ten plus years, Ashley has compiled her knowledge of her favorite fluffy creatures into this easy to read guide.

She hopes 'The Labrador Retriever Bible' will provide you with information that will aid you in having the best possible relationship you can have with your pooch.

If you gain any knowledge from this book, and think it could benefit the community, she would greatly appreciate your review on Amazon.

A Quick Guide To Dog Food Ingredients

Good For Your Dog

Whole proteins:

Chicken, Fish, Beef, Duck, Liver, Eggs

Whole grains:

Chondroitin, glucosamine, omega-3 fatty accids

Meaningful labels:

Certified organic

Natural preservatives:

Vitamin C, Vitamin E

Good fruits & vegies

Carrots, peas, sweet potatoes

Bad For Your Dog

Dangerous chemicals:

BHT ethoxyquin, BHA, proplene glycol, sodium selenite

Unspecified proteins:

'Meat-meal', 'by-products'

Unhealthy grains & fillers:

Soy, beet pulp, corn, wheat

Poorly regulated ingredients:

Products from rendering plants or from China

Bad fruits & vegies

Garlic, onions, grapes

VET/VACCINATION RECORDS

Date: _____

Age: _____

Notes: _____

_____

_____

_____

_____

Date: _____

Age: _____

Notes: _____

_____

_____

_____

_____

VET/VACCINATION RECORDS

Date: _____

Age: _____

Notes: _____

_____

_____

_____

_____

Date: _____

Age: _____

Notes: _____

_____

_____

_____

_____

VET/VACCINATION RECORDS

Date: _____

Age: _____

Notes: _____

_____

_____

_____

_____

Date: _____

Age: _____

Notes: _____

_____

_____

_____

_____

VET/VACCINATION RECORDS

Date: _____

Age: _____

Notes: _____

_____

_____

_____

_____

Date: _____

Age: _____

Notes: _____

_____

_____

_____

_____

NOTE

This book uses the male pronoun "he" to refer to "the dog". This is simply to save time and improve readability. Everything we say applies to dogs no matter the gender unless specified.

The medical information in this book is not a substitute for professional medical advice. It is intended to inform and to give you a rough idea of what you can expect in a general sense. For any issues specific to your dog, always seek the advice of professionals.

Prices quoted are based on Amazon prices at the date of publishing. Depending on your country of origin, quality requirements, luck in finding special offers, etc. these prices may vary.

PART I

PUPPY TRAINING

1

THE FIRST STEPS

So you've decided to embark on the exciting journey of dog ownership? Good for you! Having a dog in your life, when done right, is one of the most exciting experiences in the world. You will find great rewards, amazing insight, and lots of happiness all rolled up into one furry bundle. However, like most adventures, it's not something you want to embark upon lightly. A little bit of knowledge and preparation is going to save you a lot of trouble and heartache in the long run!

This book is designed to prepare you for your new life with your new puppy. It contains tips on what you need to buy and how to puppy-proof your house, exercises and games, and tons of advice for solving and preventing problems. Follow this advice and your puppy will have an excellent first year in your home – and you will have an excellent new Labrador Retriever puppy.

1.1 Choosing a puppy

. . .

Breeder or shelter?

The first thing you need to consider is whether you're going to get your puppy from a reputable breeder or look into shelters and foster homes in your area. There are arguments to be made for both cases, and we're going to look at why you would choose one over the other. Before going into that, though, there's one important thing you need to do no matter which path you take: make sure you are dealing with reputable professionals that work in full respect of the animals, the law, and health and safety regulations.

Whether it's a shelter or a breeder that you're looking for, it's always a good idea to ask for information from your local vet, kennel club or training center. They will have had contact with most of the breeders in the area and will be able to advise you on which to speak to and which to avoid. Once you have a few names, look them up online. Whether or not they have a website, it doesn't necessarily determine quality, but you might be able to find reviews about them. Don't be swayed by one good or bad review, but if there are lots of them, trust that they're there for a reason. Be especially wary of any breeder or shelter that has articles written about them online as having been abusive or neglectful. You would think that a place like that couldn't possibly stay open, but they sometimes do.

If you're looking at a breeder, look for one that specializes in your breed of choice. Most good breeders will only handle one or two breeds. Avoid the ones that claim they can get you any breed of puppy like the plague – they mostly source from puppy mills and disadvantaged countries. They should, by default, offer you all the proper documentation both for your dog and the transaction, and ensure that everything is completely above-board legally.

Your Labrador bought from a breeder must absolutely come with a pedigree and a traceable genealogy. Apart from that, look for people that are helpful and forthcoming. Great breeders offer you detailed instructions on how to care for your new puppy, as well as some tools and supplies to start you off.

If you're looking at shelters, the main thing is to be sure that you're dealing with people that do their best to treat all of their charges with kindness. Shelters should be clean and happy places. If they are keeping puppies in poor conditions, in dirty kennels or in the cold, or if the puppies look ill and under-fed, avoid at all costs. In these cases, it is also your moral obligation to immediately report what you have seen. Puppies that come from shelters should be vaccinated, micro-chipped, and in most cases, spayed or neutered. Don't even consider a shelter that lets you adopt a puppy who has never seen a veterinarian in his life.

It's also great if you can find a shelter that treats you nicely and doesn't impose unreasonable conditions. They can ask to see your residence, which is perfectly normal, but if they want to make weekly house calls for the next five years, you might want to avoid them.

Finally, how do you decide between getting your puppy from a breeder or a shelter? It's quite simple actually. You absolutely need to go to a breeder if:

- You want to participate in canine beauty shows.

- You want to compete in any canine sports at a semi-professional or professional level.

- You want to breed your dog further.

- You want your dog to do a specific job that they were

designed for: hunting, shepherding, home defense, sled pulling, etc.

- You are dead set on getting a specific breed and absolutely nothing can change your mind.

In every other condition aside from those above, you would do much better to consider adopting a puppy from a shelter or foster home.

Going to a breeder comes with advantages and disadvantages. The major advantage is that you know exactly what dog you are getting, what their health risks are, and what their family tree looks like. You can more or less tell the temperament of your future dog by looking at his ancestors. You will have a purebred dog with all the documents to testify to that, so you are free to participate in competitions or to breed it further. The disadvantages are that depending on the breed, it can cost you a lot of money. Not only will you pay a hefty sum for your puppy, but purebred dogs are also much more predisposed to genetic diseases which you will have to address with the help of a veterinarian.

Going to a shelter also has pros and cons. On the downside, your puppy will most likely be a strange mix of breeds and you won't know for sure what they are like until they grow up. However, this comes with the benefit of added health and resilience: mixed breed dogs tend to be much healthier and longer-lived. One immense advantage to getting a dog from a foster home is that they will very likely already be trained in the basics: walking on a leash and going potty outside at the very least which can save you a lot of trouble.

The greatest disadvantage is that your dog won't have a pedigree, and therefore can never take part in official competitions and shouldn't have offspring. Most of them can't since they are spayed or neutered as soon as they reach the shelter. However, if those things don't interest you anyway, then you should absolutely do a good deed and adopt a puppy that needs a home. Shelter dogs make the most intelligent, loving and rewarding pets.

Health and genetics

It's never easy to choose a puppy. Sometimes being faced with a litter of seven adorable bundles, or a shelter of dozens of wonderful dogs can be overwhelming. In the end, it's very likely that your heart will be the deciding factor in which puppy comes home with you. However, it's always a good idea to keep a couple of factors in mind, just in case you need a little extra help deciding. The important things you need to consider are genetics – in the form of health issues and breed characteristics. Let's take a look at the possibilities and why they matter.

Genetics can tell you a lot about what kind of dog your future puppy is going to grow up to be. Most importantly, people look at genetics in order to understand the potential health risks that a dog might be prone to, as well as their life expectancy and grooming needs. While breeders do their best to screen for breed-specific genetic diseases, many diseases don't actually have screening tests available. What's more, some of them occur based on complex factors, due to multiple genes as well as environmental conditions. This makes some genetic problems inevitable, and breeders should carefully screen all future breeding dogs for any signs of them – but they often don't.

Here are the most common genetic diseases that dogs

suffer from. Whether it's a Lab or any other breed you're looking at, you're likely at risk from one or two of these.

- Heart problems

Many dogs can suffer from heart problems, but the most common congenital heart disease is Mitral Valve disease. It affects very small dogs, toy breeds and older dogs, and is quite lethal. Dogs who have this problem may die due to congestive heart failure. It's very hard to identify this disease before it's too late, but you can get a good idea of your chances by looking at your puppy's ancestors, and all of his family members who are above the age of seven.

- Allergies

This is a very common problem, albeit not the most severe. If treated and kept under control, not only is it not life-threatening, it can also be unnoticeable. There are many manifestations, the most common being skin reactions such as itchiness, hot spots, and ear infections.

- Hip dysplasia

You've probably heard of this one, as it's quite a serious problem. It may not be life-threatening, but it does cause your pet severe pain and really limits their enjoyment of life. This disease can actually affect mix-breed dogs as easily as pure-bred dogs, and an estimate of 15% of all dogs suffer from it to some extent. This is one to watch out for in Labradors and any other breed that has a rounded backside.

. . .

- Knee and ligament problems

Ligament rupture is, of course, a traumatic injury, but studies have shown that there is an increased risk for certain breeds due to the development of weak spots in their tendons. It's not known to affect Labradors as much as other breeds, however, it can still occur at older ages. Knee problems are very complex and sometimes difficult to identify.

- Various other diseases

Things you might want to look out for include hereditary cancers and cataracts, as well as hypothyroidism and retained testicles. When in doubt, ask your local breeder or vet about what you can expect from each breed. Even if you're adopting a mixed-breed dog, look at his general body type and size. Is his snout shorter than usual? Is his backside rounded? Is he tiny or enormous? These things can tell you a lot about what sort of medical issues you might run into.

1.2 Before you bring your puppy home

So you've decided on a puppy, and are just waiting for him to be ready to join you. Excellent! This is the perfect time to stop, look around yourself, and honestly evaluate how prepared you really are. A new life in the house is going to be a huge disturbance to everybody and everything, so it's better if you know exactly what to expect ahead of time. There are lots of things you can do to prepare yourself, your family and your home, as well as lots of supplies you will need.

. . .

What to expect from your new puppy

Many first-time dog owners aren't really prepared for what a puppy entails. Many experienced owners are also surprised since it's very easy to forget those rough first six months in the joy of what comes after. Various breeds have various needs, but puppies all have one thing in common: they demand a lot of attention and time. Ideally, you would have at least one weekend, if not a whole week, in which you have nothing else to do other than acclimatize your new puppy. Schedule his arrival in such a way that you don't just dump him in the house and go to work since that can be very traumatizing for a young dog.

Consider the fact that he has just been removed from his family and from everything he has known for his entire life. You should expect him to take a week to adjust to his new environment. It's also reasonable to assume that there will be a lot of barking and whining in the beginning, so you should talk to any neighbors and smooth things over in advance.

Puppies do sleep quite a bit. You can expect several hour-long naps throughout the day, as well as a full night of sleep if you educate him properly. However, when they are not sleeping, puppies are extremely active, curious and energetic. If left to their own devices, they can cause massive amounts of trouble in a very short amount of time, and will never give you a moment of peace.

In terms of exercise, more is better. A tired puppy is a happy puppy and has a happy owner. You should prepare for two walks a day, morning and evening, when his energy levels are going to be at their highest. You will also need one to two hours of active play (fetch, tug, chase) distributed throughout the day, and an hour of obedience training divided into 10-minute sessions throughout the day. Don't be surprised if you don't get much done in those first few weeks.

While adult dogs do tend to mellow down with age, you will still need to put in almost the same amount of time. The difference is that adult dogs have much higher stamina so you can do fewer sessions that last longer. Instead of two short walks a day, you can have a nice hour-long walk in the morning and that will be fine. Add to that a good half hour of fetch and games, and you will satisfy most Labradors.

Puppies also need a lot of company. Don't expect that you will be able to leave him alone for 8 hours straight on his third day. If you work, you have to consider either puppy daycare, bringing him with you, hiring someone to come feed and play with the puppy at lunchtime, or coming home during lunch hour yourself. A puppy left alone for that long can develop serious mental issues, as well as destroy most of the furniture in the house.

Supplies you will need

There are an enormous amount of tools, toys, and treats available for dogs. It can be overwhelming if you walk into the pet store without a list. Most first-time puppy owners are guilty of over-spending and over-buying gadgets that they will never use. The following is a complete, comprehensive list of those things which you are absolutely going to make use of sooner or later. While some can be bought along the way, it's a lot better to just get everything in place before the new puppy arrives.

. . .

1. A crate that is large enough to fit your future adult dog + a way to divide it down to the size of your puppy.

Rather than buying a small crate for your puppy and then buying another one later, be a smart shopper and get one sized for your future dog. You can always use a separator to make the space smaller so that it doesn't feel too intimidating for your new pup, and to prevent him from going potty inside it. A crate is an absolute life-saver. It is the one and only safe way to transport your dog in the car, it can make potty training and sleep training much easier, it provides him with a safe space to retreat to, and it can give you some peace of mind. Say you have an emergency, and the puppy has to stay with the vet or come with you in the car for many hours? He can stay in his crate. Say you spilled something dangerous on the floor and need to prevent him from touching it while you clean? He can stay in his crate. Crates can help with separation anxiety, visits to the vet, and a whole host of other problems. We will be using them frequently throughout the training exercises in this book, so you absolutely need one.

2. A good quality harness, collar, and leash.

The leash is self-explanatory. Avoid the plastic retractable ones as they tend to teach your dog the bad habit of pulling, which is not what you want unless you're getting a husky in the future. Get a nice strong, lightweight leash that is 5 feet (1.5 meters) long. You should get both a harness and a collar, regardless of which you will choose to use with your dog when he is an adult. With a puppy, you have to use the harness for at least six months while he's still just barely learning to walk by your side. Even after that, it can be a great training tool, and useful for holding a puppy still during vet and groomer visits. You should also get a collar and keep it on your puppy at all times when outside, even though the leash will be attached to the harness. The collar should have an ID tag with your phone number on it so that if the worst should happen and your puppy escapes from his harness, anyone who finds him can call you right away. A collar is also a training tool you will use a lot in the future, so have a good quality, preferably leather one. It should be flat and have an adjustable size. Initially, it should fit on your puppy's neck snugly enough that you can put one finger under it comfortably, no more than that.

3. Bowls, food and hygiene products.

Buy two stainless steel bowls for food and water. Be sure to wash these regularly even if they seem clean. Buy enough good quality puppy food to last you a month, preferably the same variety that the breeder was using if possible. It's also a good idea to invest in some delicious healthy treats such as freeze-dried liver or heart. We will talk more about nutrition later in this book, but for now, just remember that most treats are junk food and should not be used by any responsible dog parent. Consider your puppy's hygiene needs. Will he need a specific kind of brush for grooming? Get that. Buy a large bottle of a natural, hypoallergenic dog shampoo – don't be afraid to spend a bit more on this item, since you will be using very little of it and it will last you a very long time. If you intend to clip nails yourself, get a dog-specific nail clipper. You can also buy toothpaste and a toothbrush, but it will be much easier to finger brush at first. There is more information on grooming later on in the book, and it includes instructions on nail clipping and tooth brushing.

. . .

4. Toys.

Don't go crazy getting complex toys as puppies are only going to chew through them. You need a variety of very simple toys with different textures in order to find out what your dog likes best. A great pack to start with would be: a dog-safe rubber bouncy ball to play fetch with, a rope to play tug with, and something soft tied to a durable string for chasing games. Make sure that all of these toys will fit in your dog's mouth, but are not small enough that he could choke on them. The other important thing you need to invest in right now is chew toys. Each dog has different preferences, but they all like to chew, so unless you're willing to sacrifice your slippers or the couch, you need to offer alternatives. A good selection of chew toys should include a natural rawhide bone, an antler or some other hard natural bone, a medium strength Nylabone or similar toy, a medium strength rubber teething ring, and a puppy Kong. Absolutely avoid any toys which are stuffed, or which have squeakers. Rest assured that your puppy will have more than enough predatory and destructive drive without these added stimuli.

5. Other small essentials.

Depending on your local ordinances, you may have an obligation to have a muzzle with you at all times when you are walking the dog in public, even if it's just in your pocket. A cheap, soft textile muzzle will more than suffice for this purpose, and you can also use it whenever you visit the vet. Buy a large supply of doggy waste baggies, as you will likely be using them frequently. Invest in a good quality bottle of enzyme cleaner for when your puppy has accidents in the house, as none of your current cleaning supplies will get rid of the smell, and your puppy will attempt to pee in the same spot again. Chlorine actually makes the problem worse rather than better and the only thing that works is an enzyme cleaning solution. Don't fall for the lure of bitter apple deterrent spray, good training and obedience is all you need. You can also buy bedding, but it's probably going to get destroyed more than once during the first few months so you're better off using towels and old sweaters if you have them. If you want your dog to pee outside, absolutely do not buy pee pads. It's much better to train him to go where you want him to from the very first day.

Preparing your home

Now that you have everything you need, and you know more or less what you can expect, it's time to puppy-proof the house. This doesn't have to be a painful process, but it will involve you getting used to keeping a tidy home as everything left lying about can be a target for misadventure.

The absolute most important thing you have to do is make sure that the entire house is safe for a puppy, even the areas where you don't think he will be allowed. Big wobbly items of furniture should be secured or removed. All power cables should be raised, hidden, or at the very least tied down when the other options aren't possible. Shoes and remote controls should have their own places, out of reach or behind closed doors. Anything that's valuable or very dear to you should be safely stowed above-puppy level. Take special care to not keep books or other documents at floor level. It might also be a good idea to put any expensive, well-loved carpets away for a while, and only take them back out in 6 to 8 months.

If you have a yard, check the fencing. If there's a gap that your puppy could squeeze through, he absolutely will. If you intend to let him play outside without your supervision, invest in some chicken wire to reinforce the inside of all of your fences until your dog has grown. It may not be pretty, but it's only temporary. Add a layer of chicken wire to the inside of any balconies or terraces that have large gaps a puppy could fall through.

This would be a good time to decide where the puppy will spend time when unsupervised. If you were thinking of setting him down in the living room and letting him run loose, think again. That's a recipe for trouble, destroyed furniture, anger, and a ruined relationship. Try to set aside space where he can spend time with absolutely no chance of destroying anything of yours. This safe space can be a small room, or a corner of the living room fenced off by a playpen. Playpens don't cost a lot of money and are well worth it for your peace of mind.

Place his crate – divided to be just the right size for him – in this puppy space, and put bedding inside it. A good trick is to put one of your dirty shirts in there for the puppy, as having your smell nearby will help keep him calm at night. Expect any bedding you place in here to potentially be destroyed. Set down his food and water bowls. He should have fresh water available at all times until dinnertime, and food only on a regular schedule.

His toys should be divided into two categories: the play toys, such as the ball, tug toy, chase toy, frisbee, etc., which should be placed in a box well out of reach; and his chew toys: kong, bones, antlers, etc., which should be available to him in his playpen at all times. Don't ever take his chew toys away from him, he should be encouraged to have one in his mouth constantly.

Finally, and most importantly, prepare your family members. Young children should receive special instructions on how to behave with the puppy. If you want to avoid trouble, bite wounds, visits to the ER and other catastrophes, children should be expressly forbidden from ever jumping on the dog, shouting at the dog, pulling his ears or tail, wrestling with him, picking him up, or even running around him. The puppy is not a toy. As much as your children would love to pick him up and walk around the entire house with him in their arms, one stumble can lead to a broken paw and a permanently damaged dog. Avoid the scenario in which the puppy is tired, grumpy, has had a rough day, and is being pestered by the kids while he's trying to sleep. This can easily turn into a nasty bite from even the most benevolent of puppies. Puppies have incredibly sharp teeth in order to make up for being small and weak, don't underestimate them.

Remember to instruct everyone in the family that any items left lying around on the floor where the puppy can reach them are fair game and will be destroyed. What's more, kid's toys are a choking hazard for dogs and should be very carefully put away. Decide on ground rules that you all agree on and have to keep. Will the puppy be allowed on the couch? On the bed? Who is responsible for feeding and training him? Where will he sleep? The rules only work if everyone in the family agrees to them, otherwise, your puppy will very quickly learn who to turn to when he wants special treatment.

Congratulations, you're done! Your house and family are now ready for the new puppy. You have all the supplies you could possibly need, and you have a plan for how to care for him. You're about to start a wonderful journey and experience your first day with your new best friend!

. . .

1.3 The first day

Starting off on the right foot

It's important to start off on the right foot with your new puppy from day one. The rules you set now are going to set you up for success later on, so you should already know exactly what they are. Don't allow your puppy to do anything that you don't want him to do for the rest of his life. At this early stage, habits form quickly. We've all seen those hilarious photos of Great Danes who think they are still puppies and insist on sleeping on their owner's lap, but it's not so funny when it happens to you.

While the first day is not about training, you do want to start getting your puppy used to his environment. Start by placing him in his designated potty area, and spending some time there. If you're lucky, having just gotten there from a long trip, he might decide to use the facilities. This would be a great time to break out the treats and throw him a party!

Throughout the day, every time you see your puppy unconsciously doing something good, such as going potty outside, sitting, checking out his crate, drinking from his bowl or chewing on one of his readily available chew toys, make a huge fuss about rewarding him. Praise, cuddle, and give treats like there's no tomorrow! By just doing this, you're already setting yourself up for success.

Try not to overwhelm your puppy as soon as he gets home. Get family members to greet the puppy quietly, one at a time, and limit play sessions to 15 minutes. Puppies get tired quickly and need to take breaks often, and tired puppies get grumpy and mean. Try to do your regular daily activities around him as much as possible – cooking and eating dinner, for example. Feel free to put him in his crate for naps, but keep his crate nearby at all times so that he can be close to you. He just got separated from his family, so he needs the company! Imagine that he is a small alien and you are showing him what a day in the life of a human is all about. Everything you show him now is going to be one less thing to stress him out later!

When he meets new people, get them to give him treats. Make sure every interaction is a happy one so that he will get used to you, your family, your neighbors, and strangers. We hope to cultivate a puppy that is trusting and loving, not one that is afraid of people.

Have little play sessions throughout the day. It's a rule with dogs that while they are playing, they aren't stressed or afraid. Those feelings are mutually exclusive. By playing tug or chase, you give him a chance to blow off steam and relax. If your puppy is refusing to play at all, it could be a sign that he is stressed out. Start by removing all other people from the equation – especially children. If the puppy tries to retreat from a game, kids are very likely to grab him and drag him back where he doesn't want to be. You have to prevent this from happening at all costs. A stressed, tired and angry puppy is very likely to develop negative associations with the cause of his stress – in this case, little people. An adult dog who is aggressive towards children is a huge problem and a possible cause for euthanasia, so don't give him the chance to grow annoyed with them now.

Take him out to his potty area often. Later on in the book, we have a step by step potty guide, but for now, just be prepared that you will have to take him out very often on the first few days. Unless you have specifically seen him go potty, watch him like a hawk. He should not have free range of the house. If you have seen him go, then you can relax for about two hours.

Make sure his sleeping arrangements for that first night are comfortable. It's going to be a nightmare for both of you, either way, so be prepared, but do your best to make it easier on him. Start, on day one, by getting him to sleep where you intend for him to sleep for the rest of his life, be it in a crate, on a bed in his playpen, in a different room, next to your bed, or anywhere else. Remember, there is no such thing as "it's just this once" in dog language. Once he's on your bed, it will take massive amounts of effort to deprogram that.

Set your alarm to wake up at least twice during the night to take him out to potty. If he's whining and barking, take him out to the potty area, but don't let him do anything else – no playing, no jumping up on the bed, no cuddles. If he goes – good; if not, he has to go right back to his bed anyway. Be strong. Don't give in to complaining. It will take a few days for him to get used to sleeping alone, so be prepared to have a few rough nights ahead of you. Placing one of your dirty shirts in his bedding can help, that way he can smell that you are near. Enjoy your first day. It will be rough, but it will get better!

Punishment and reward

Rewarding your dog is as simple as it gets – though many people still manage to get it wrong. However, punishment is a tricky issue – there are those who say it should never be done. That is only partially accurate. It should never be done in anger, aggressively or violently. The right kind of punishment given at the right time is one of the most powerful educational tools in your arsenal.

What kind of punishment is acceptable, then? There are two major kinds of punishment which you can apply to a dog. Either you are adding something to the equation, which is called "positive punishment", or you are removing something from the equation, which is called "negative punishment".

An example of positive punishment is that your puppy is about to start chewing on your favorite slipper. You go to him and firmly but calmly tell him "no". You just added your voice, tone, and presence to the situation. Once a dog understands the concept of "no", that will be enough positive punishment 99% of the time.

An example of negative punishment is that your puppy got too aggressive while he was playing with you and bit you too hard. You calmly pick him up and put him in his pen, where he has to stay in time-out for the next half an hour. You just denied him the freedom to roam around the house and play with you – that too is a form of punishment and a very potent one.

Of the two, negative punishment is surprisingly the most powerful and, at the same time, has the least chance of scarring or upsetting your puppy. It's what we're going to use most of the time in order to transmit to our puppy that certain behavior is not acceptable. Here is an amazing exercise that you can play with your puppy starting from the first day that will already introduce to him (and you) the concepts of "yes", "no", reward, and punishment.

Puppy's first reward and punishment exercise.

You're going to need your puppy, a comfortable carpet to sit on, and a large bagful of delicious treats. This exercise also works really well with your puppy's regular kibble if

ry (and they always are). Just substitute giving
lar meal with this exercise, keeping track of how
le you give him.

Step 1. Get down on the floor. Your puppy is likely going to
come to you and check you out immediately. If not, be
patient. When he does give you his attention, say "yes"
happily and give him a treat.

Step 2. Your puppy is likely paying attention to you now. If
he drifts away, either be patient or make a little noise to get
him to look at you. When he does, say "yes" and reward
him again. If he keeps his attention on you without getting
distracted, keep rewarding him. We are simply teaching
the pup that we like it when he pays attention to us, and
that whenever he hears the word "yes", good things
happen.

Feel free to repeat the first two steps and leave it at that for
the first few sessions. It may not seem like much, but
teaching your puppy that it's good when he pays attention
to you is a huge deal.

Step 3. When you feel ready, put a treat in your hand.
Make sure he sees that you did it. Close your fist around
that treat and offer your closed fist to your puppy. Make
sure he doesn't get the treat. This may hurt a little –
puppies have very sharp teeth, and it's likely he's going to
dig and claw at your hand to get to the treat. While he is
doing this, gently and calmly say "no."

Step 4. Wait. Be patient. If he is still digging at your hand
after a minute, gently and calmly say "no" again.
Remember that at this point he doesn't know what it
means, so he won't respond to it. We are teaching him by
using negative punishment – we are denying him access to
the treat that he wants.

Step 5. If you are lucky, it will only take a few seconds for your puppy to give up digging at your hand. If you are very lucky, he will then look at you to figure out what's next. When he does that, say "yes", open your fist, give him the treat, and shower him in treats and praise like it's his birthday.

Repeat steps three to five multiple times. Take a break, then repeat them again after an hour. Sooner or later, depending on how smart your puppy is, he will understand that the treat only comes when he stops chewing your hand and looks at you. When you can tell that he got it and it only takes him a second to get there, celebrate!

You have just taught your puppy to pay attention to you, and more specifically, to pay attention to your face rather than your hand. You have just taught him that when you make the sound "no", the good thing doesn't happen. But when you make the sound "yes!", it does! These are the fundamental things that you will need moving forward.

Repeat this exercise often and for a very long time. Don't assume that just because he got the idea of "yes" and "no" in this context, he will know them everywhere else. Don't start throwing them around expecting things to happen. These are just the fundamental building blocks that you will use to construct respect and understanding between yourself and your puppy.

Other important first day occasions to start practicing reward and punishment.

Aside from the above exercise, there will be many situations in which you can and should practice reward and punishment, starting with the very first day. You should be stalking your new puppy like a hawk, ready to take advantage of any situation in which you can educate him.

If you're lucky and he goes potty as soon as you get him in the yard, that's a huge milestone and should be rewarded heavily. For the next six months, every time he goes potty in the right place, you should throw him a party. Praise is good, but treats are better, so have them on hand or stash them safely in the yard where you can reach them.

If you have an excitable pup who goes nuts whenever you're about to open the door or to set the food bowl down, practice negative punishment by making him wait. You're essentially saying "no, you don't get this thing that you want until you calm down." When he is no longer jumping up on the door or on you, you can reward him by doing what he wanted: opening the door or setting down the food bowl.

A word of warning: you have to be very patient and very careful. If you give him what he wants while he is still acting badly, you are going to reinforce his belief that that's the right way to behave.

For example: You are on the couch. The puppy is on the floor but wants to join you. He starts barking and whining.

What you should NEVER do: Go "ok, fine, just as long as you shut up" and pick him up on the couch. You will end up with a dog that barks at you and orders you around whenever he wants anything at all, and this could potentially escalate into dangerous, aggressive behavior.

What you should do: Pretend he's invisible as long as he's barking. Be patient. Wait for an hour, if that's what it takes. If you do anything to shut him up right now, you are going to get much worse barking later. When he finally stops and settles down, you can pick him up.

Another great way to use negative punishment is to enforce a time-out. This is especially useful for puppies which tend to play too rough or bite too hard. Whenever he becomes too excited and can't be calmed down, give him a five-minute time-out in his playpen or crate. By denying him the right to continue playtime, you are punishing him for going overboard.

These are all actions that will build up to solid foundations in the long run. They are not quick fixes and one time-out will not make your hyper puppy permanently calm. But there is no such thing as a quick-fix for good behavior. Invest in your puppy's education now and you won't regret it when you have a loving, patient, calm, well-behaved adult dog.

Discipline and rules

Now that you know the "how" of enforcing discipline, it's time to talk about what exactly discipline is going to mean to you and your dog. When we say "discipline", most people think of army uniforms, black boots, waking up at five in the morning, and shouting. But this isn't about giving your puppy, or yourself, a hard time. This is about setting rules and boundaries in such a way that you can develop a happy relationship without the risk of misunderstandings, anger, and trauma.

While it's nice to remember that our puppies are related to magnificent wild animals such as wolves and jackals, it is also important to remember that they are only very distantly related. Our pups have been bred for thousands of years to be what they are, from the moment the first wolf took a piece of fried meat from the first hunter. They are designed to live with us, work with us, and most importantly, to cooperate with us. A dog that does not have a role in the family, does not know his place, and does not have a job, is an unhappy, unsatisfied dog.

You may have seen the classic case of the Jack Russel Terrier who thinks he is the owner of the house. He attacks visitors, barks at the television, demands to sleep on his owner's pillow, and growls if you go near his toy. Some people would say he is only being a dog, doing what is naturally his instinct to do. That's absolutely wrong. A dog living under those conditions is constantly stressed out and miserable. He doesn't feel safe in his own family because there's nobody there to take charge – so he has to do it. Even though he doesn't like it.

A dog that does not live under a framework of discipline is always an unhappy dog. No matter how kind-hearted you are and how adorable your puppy is, you have to remember that you need to do the hard work for his well being, and for the well being of your family. We have no doubts that discipline and education are quintessential for young children, and yet many puppy owners assume that the same isn't true for puppies. Complete freedom is a recipe for disaster in both cases, but by setting reasonable rules and maintaining discipline, you can have a happy and balanced household.

The actual rules change from case to case, from owner to owner. Nobody has the right to tell you what you are or are not allowed to do with your own dog. Behaviors that are acceptable to some families may not be acceptable to others. Whatever you choose, you're the one who is going to have to live with it. There are some universal rules and there are some that you will have to decide for yourself. In both cases, the time to start enforcing them is now, on day one. Don't allow your puppy to do things that you don't intend to allow him to do forever. Dogs don't understand the concept of "it's a special occasion" or "it's just until he grows up."

Universal rules for a disciplined puppy

1. It is never ok for the puppy to bark, bite, whine, or growl to get what he wants. Ever. This is an immediate cause for negative punishment. This includes begging for food, toys, treats, coming up on the couch, or even just getting your attention. Never give in to puppy manipulation. Reward calm, civilized behavior only. The one exception? If he's whining at the door because he needs to pee. That's usually considered a great thing!

2. It is never ok for the puppy to chew objects other than his designated, puppy-safe chews. Remove the object in question immediately, replace it with an appropriate toy, and praise him for chewing on his toys.

3. It is never ok for the puppy to attack other people or dogs, not even if he's "jealous" because you are interacting with them and not him. It's not cute, it's dangerous behavior. This should be cause for an immediate time-out.

4. It is never ok for the puppy to decide when and how much he eats. It doesn't matter if he looks like he's always hungry, you know better. Most puppies will eat until they vomit if allowed. There's a chapter later on about nutrition and obesity which will help you figure out how much food he needs. Stick to that measurement. Don't ever allow a puppy to bully you into putting down a bowl of food. Wait until he is calm and do it on your own terms.

5. A disciplined puppy must allow you to touch him. This includes his paws, his belly, his tail, looking inside his ears,

opening his mouth, and looking at his teeth. This is not something that will just happen overnight: you have to take the time to do it, a little at a time, every single day until it becomes completely natural. You have to be able to groom your puppy, check for injuries, check his dental health, administer medication, and lots of other things. If you can't touch him, you can't help him when he needs it, so this rule isn't up for debate.

Personal rules that you get to decide

1. Where will he be sleeping? The best possible option would be a comfortable, correctly sized crate. Even if he complains at first, adult dogs love having their den to which they can retreat to get some peace and quiet. Second best would be a doggie bed. You can place it inside his play-pen to still have some control at night – not as much as a crate gives you, but enough. Worst on the list would be your bed. This may still work for shy, submissive dogs, but it's an absolute nightmare if your dog happens to be stubborn and dominant. He could easily decide that because he sleeps next to you, he is just as important as you in the pack, or more so.

2. Where is his potty area? Most people recommend outside on the grass. Depending on your situation and your pup, puppy pads are not to be excluded completely. They could be a fine option in an apartment or in a high-rise. Wherever it is, pick one and stick to it.

3. Who will be the primary trainer and educator of the puppy? Of course, a disciplined dog will obey anyone in the family, but there should always be one person who gets the final word. Think of this scenario: you are out with your family and puppy. He wiggles out of his harness and

starts gunning it for the road. Cars are passing at high speed. You all panic. Some of your family members yell "Stop!", others yell "Come here!" from three different directions. Your puppy needs to know, in a split second, whose voice is the one he actually obeys. It can be a matter of life and death.

4. Is he allowed up on the couch? The chairs? The table? The kitchen counter? No? Then don't ever allow him to even consider going on there. If he's been on it once, he will consider it his right to go there again. Is he allowed up on your lap? Consider this one wisely. Refusing to let a puppy sleep on your lap is one of the hardest things a new dog owner can do, but when that puppy grows up and weighs more than you do, regrets quickly sink in.

5. What are your leash walking goals? Do you consider him well disciplined if he only pulls a little and then comes back? If he never reaches the end of the leash, but within that limit walks freely? Or will you only be satisfied if he walks in "heel" position all the time? While the "heel" position is harder to train, it is absolutely possible, and in some cases necessary – such as when being walked by an elderly person or a pregnant woman. Some dog breeds take to it more than others. Normally, moderation is best in these situations – the walk has to be fun for your dog too.

6. Where will he have access once the potty-training phase is complete? It's perfectly fine to keep some rooms as dog-free zones. It might be a great idea for the children's room, for example. Perhaps you want to keep him out of the second floor of the house. One thing should be very clear, however – if you intend to get a dog to keep exclusively in the yard, potentially tied to a dog-house, don't. That's not an acceptable life for any dog and most countries are working on eliminating that primitive practice. Most shel-

ters won't even let you adopt a dog unless you guarantee that it gets to be in the house, with the family.

It's a good idea to keep these rules in mind or even write them down on paper. It's inevitable that some will change as your puppy grows older and you begin to understand what you expect from each other. However, you still need to start from somewhere, right from the first day.

Now that you know how to praise and punish your puppy, to teach him the foundations of the concepts of "yes" and "no", and what exactly your discipline goals are, you're ready to take your first few days head-on. There will be more detailed instructions for specific categories such as obedience or potty training later on, but they all use the same basic concepts that we've already explored in this section. Practice rewarding your puppy whenever he does something good and finding an appropriate punishment when you don't like his behavior. Never punish him in anger. There's no point, you're only going to frighten him and ruin your relationship. Instead, be an educator and work with him towards your discipline goals.

The Vet – vaccines, microchips, and neutering.

Your final consideration for this big day is booking an appointment with your vet for a regular health check-up, as well as any planned future interventions such as vaccination. Depending on your situation and where your puppy comes from, he may (and should) already be vaccinated, micro-chipped, and potentially spayed or neutered. If he's not, this has to be done as soon as possible. Let's look at your options and obligations.

Finding a vet shouldn't be too hard. Most of the time, unless you have a specific reason to avoid him, your local town vet is a safe bet. Make sure he's nice and make sure he's always available. He should have an emergency number for when he's off duty. If something happens to your pup in the middle of the night, he has to be available. It will cost you, but you need to have that option. Also, it might be a good idea to find a backup vet in case anything happens to your primary one.

Vaccines are mandatory in most places in the world and for good reason. There are many horrible ways in which your puppy could get sick from viruses and bacteria, often passed to him by unvaccinated dogs through something as brief as a sniff. Some are carried by mosquitoes, ticks, or fleas. There's no reason to take any chances as they cost very little, only need to be topped off once a year, and have absolutely no harmful side-effects. Don't fall for the hype: there's no such thing as over-vaccinating.

Most vets are going to give your puppy his first set of shots around three months of age, so book them now. They also recommend that you should avoid taking him out in public until they have had all of their shots, which can be as late as six months time, but that's actually impossible. You need to start on leash training and socialization. A dog that is separated from the world for the first six months of his life is going to be dysfunctional to a lesser or greater extent forever. One option is to use your yard if you have one, and invite friends over with dogs which you know are healthy and vaccinated. You could also take walks on quieter, more isolated streets. One thing is true, you should probably avoid large crowds as much as possible, and especially avoid meeting any stray dogs until you've had the full range of shots.

Micro-chipping is also mandatory in most countries and even if it isn't, it's a good idea. Hundreds of dogs are rescued every day and sent back to their loving families thanks to being microchipped. Harnesses can break, tags can fall off, but that chip is forever. The procedure takes an instant, it hurts about as much as a bee sting (which your puppy will surely experience more than once in his life), and is completely safe. Many shelters also offer help to people who can't afford the cost of the procedure and some will even do it for free.

As for spaying or neutering, it tends to be a big debate, but it's really a very simple question. If you got your puppy at a shelter, he's probably already neutered. It's standard procedure and has helped reduce the number of stray dogs in recent years more than any other practice. If he's not, the decision is ultimately yours, but here's a rough guideline:

- You absolutely have to do it if your dog has any sort of genetic disease or is at high risk for any sort of genetic disease. You have to do it if he needs it for health reasons – such as ovarian tumors.

- You don't have to, but still probably should do it if you don't know your dog's genetic background and suspect it might be dubious. This is the case for most shelter dogs. You should also do it if your dog tends to be an escape artist and you live in a community where most people don't spay or neuter, like most villages. The goal here is to avoid putting more unsound, unhealthy, unwanted puppies out into the world.

- You don't have to do it if you are sure that your dog is genetically sound, is secure on your property, and has zero health risks related to his reproductive organs.

- You absolutely must not do it if you intend to breed your dog or have him participate in any sports or breed competitions.

Remember that this is not about you and your pride. This is about what's best for your dog and for your community. If you have doubts about neutering your dog, just go visit the local shelter and see how many unwanted dogs are still in the world. Many shelters still have to kill the animals that don't get adopted quickly enough.

As for the rumors that dogs become slow, fat, and lazy after they get neutered: that's completely false. Yes, his dietary needs may change a little bit and it's your job to adjust for that. An obese dog is the fault of the owner, not of neutering. If you keep your dog fit, healthy, and active, he will remain fit, healthy, and active his whole life. The evidence that dogs "calm down" after neutering is circumstantial: Most dogs are neutered between six months and one year of age. That's roughly around when they would naturally start to calm down no matter what you do to them. It's part of the process of growing up. That's also why neutering is never a solution to a hyperactive, aggressive pet. It won't even stop him from humping your leg. The only thing it changes is his ability to create unwanted puppies destined for the shelter.

A HEALTHY, HAPPY DOG

2.1 Potty training

It's a good idea to start thinking about potty training as soon as your new puppy walks in the door. It may not be as life-saving as a good recall, or as fun to show to your friends as a solid roll over, but going potty is going to be a big deal to the both of you, so you should know how to do it right.

Potty training is the one part of your dog's education that will take the longest time before showing any result at all, and often times it can seem like you're taking more steps backward than forward. Most owners go through several bottles of enzyme cleaner and multiple carpets before they can breathe a sigh of relief – and that only comes around the time your puppy is one year old. However, if you don't take steps towards teaching your dog when and where to go potty, it won't come at all. So let's get started!

. . .

Absolute rules you have to follow

- Clean all potty "accidents" with enzyme cleaner only. Absolutely no bleach or household cleaners, they will only make matters worse.

- If you discover an "accident" after it's already been done, do not punish your puppy. This is extremely important. Bringing your puppy to the scene of the crime, shouting, showing him what he did will absolutely NOT work. You will damage your relationship, hurt the puppy, and achieve nothing. Clean the area carefully and move on. This rule is firm. If you can't obey it, you might as well invest in puppy diapers because you're going to be here for a very long time.

- If you catch your puppy in the middle of "going" on the carpet, remove him calmly and without anger to his designated potty area. Do not shout, do not shake the puppy, do not punish him in any way. You are an educator, not a source of danger for your puppy.

- If you catch your puppy "going" in the right place, you must reward him heavily. Keep his treats handy at all times, stash some in your pockets, stash some near his potty place. Don't get caught without treats.

- Do not purposefully allow your puppy to go potty in the wrong place. Many owners think they can get away with letting him potty indoors while they are at work, but teaching him to go outdoors the rest of the time. Or letting him go indoors "just until he grows up". This will not work. You have to make alternative arrangements for when you are away. There should only be one correct potty place and he should always use that place.

· · ·

How to start potty training

We've already talked about this, but it bears repeating: as soon as you bring your new puppy home, bring him to his potty area first before anything else happens. Let him hang out there with no distractions for a bit. With a bit of luck, you will have your first chance to reward him right away!

The system is very simple from then onward. You have to watch your puppy like a hawk. Soon you will start to recognize his patterns: sniffing the ground, heading for corners or carpets, circling around the same spot a few times. If you manage to catch him in time, take him out to his potty spot and praise his success!

Now that you're sure your puppy just went potty, you can breathe a sigh of relief and maybe let him play by himself, chew a bone, or hang out in his playpen for an hour or two. After that, you have to go back to watching him like a hawk! You can expect your puppy to need to pee once every three to five hours, depending on his size. If he's eating the right food, in the right quantity, and of the right quality, he should be pooping as many times a day as he is eating – most commonly that will be twice a day. The good thing about puppies is that usually, when food goes in, within the next ten minutes, they will also need to poop. This gives you a lot of control over making sure that he goes where you want him to.

You can't leave a puppy by himself for more than a few hours for the first month of his life with you. Not if you want to educate him quickly and efficiently. If there's nobody at home while you're at work, be prepared to ask or hire someone to stop by for a potty and play break once or twice a day.

· · ·

5+ hours alone during the day

It's not ideal, but it's a situation that realistically can happen. Everyone in your family works full-time, and you can't find anyone to visit him this week, and there's no puppy daycare in your area, and none of your friends like puppies. Aside from needing new friends, you're also going to need some sort of solution for him to go potty while you're away.

In these situations, a puppy playpen is absolutely mandatory. A crate is too restrictive and having free roam of the house has too many variables, so you need to place him in a playpen where he has access to his bed, water, chew toys, and a potty area.

This potty area has to fulfill two requirements: it has to be on the opposite side of the pen from his bed, as he will try to "go" as far away from his bed as possible; and it has to be made of the same material as his normal potty area.

If you normally want him to go outside on the grass, you're in luck! You can easily set up a potty system for him indoors by filling a plastic or disposable aluminum tray with litter or puppy pee pads and covering it with a large enough square of either turf or fake grass. You can get everything you need in any home improvement store cheaply. The same goes for gravel-going puppies! Cover the litter or puppy pee pads with the same gravel you have outside in his potty area.

It's really not a good idea to use just plain puppy pee pads or newspapers. Once a dog gets used to a certain sound and texture, he will always want to use the same one. It's much better to start off with the right texture from day one.

. . .

Going potty at night

Puppies have small bladders and this can normally last up until around six months of age, but it varies from puppy to puppy.

The absolute best thing to do is to train him to sleep in a crate at night. Dogs are den animals and they have the instinct to never soil where they sleep if they can help it. The space he has in his crate should be just enough for him to stand up, sit, lie down, and curl up. If the crate is any larger than that, you will have to divide it into smaller sections. It's not meant to be a luxury villa, just a bed for the night.

Crate training your puppy has hundreds of advantages, including helping you potty train. While he's young, you will have to close the door to the crate at night so that he has to vocalize and ask you when he needs to go potty. When they are older, crate-trained dogs love to go sleep in their safe, snug crates at night, and you can even leave the door open for them. Once they have these good habits ingrained, they never lose them!

Teach your puppy to love his crate slowly by rewarding him for each step. Throw treats inside and let him chase them. Have him sit inside and reward him through the door. Let him come back out, throw a toy inside, and reward him for chasing it. In short, make him feel completely comfortable with his crate. Only close the door for a few seconds and reward him again. Take it slowly and make him think that his crate is the best place on earth!

In the evening, remove his water bowl right after dinner. If he keeps drinking right until he goes to bed, you will end up getting up much more often than you'd like. He will not become dehydrated if he doesn't have any water available

between seven p.m. and seven a.m.! When yo
go to bed, take him to his crate and throw some ..
a delicious chewy toy inside. With luck, he will be
thrilled by the bedding and so eager to chew he won't even
notice you closing the door.

If he whines right away, don't give in. Of course, he would
rather be sleeping on the bed, on your pillow, but that's not
where a good puppy belongs. Don't give in to him manipu-
lating you and complaining. If you open that crate door
even once while he's whining, he will immediately understand that whining makes you open the door and he will
never stop doing it.

However, it's very important that you keep the crate somewhere where you can hear him during the night. If he
settles down, falls asleep, and then wakes up and cries,
that's a sure sign that he has to go right away! Take him to
his potty area and praise him wildly if he uses the facilities.
Then take him right back to his crate.

Even if he doesn't cry out, it's a good idea to set your
alarm clock to wake you up twice during the first few
nights and take him out. If you notice that he seems happy
to go only once and then sleep through the rest of the
night, adjust your alarm accordingly. If you're lucky, within
a week or two, it's even possible that going once very late
right before bed and once very early in the morning will be
enough!

Adult dogs can easily hold it for an entire night with no
problem and if they're well educated to sleep in their crate
and go potty outside, you will never have to worry about a
thing.

What to expect from a normal day

.o the rhythm of when your puppy
ome second nature to you. Here's a
ιen you can expect an average puppy,
to need to go potty if you follow our
ιrned what's expected of him:

ι wake up in the morning, before anything
else, μ˅   ak.

- Breakfast at the same hour each morning and another potty break five to fifteen minutes after.

- If the puppy is "empty", relax for a few hours.

- Around five months, you can expect a potty break every three to four hours.

- Dinner at the same hour each day, a potty break five to fifteen minutes after. Remove water bowl.

- Last potty break before going to bed, say ten p.m.

- One potty break during the night, say three a.m.

It may seem like quite a bit at first, but having a puppy is a huge commitment. This schedule can and should be divided among multiple people, including yourself, your family, your neighbors, a professional dog sitter/walker, a puppy daycare, or friends who want to help. Unless you work from home, it won't be possible to properly potty train your puppy.

Of course, if you can't do this, it's not the end of the world. Your puppy may learn to go outside long before being six months old with the right care, or it may take him two years if you don't have the time. Follow this advice as much as you possibly can for both your benefit, but don't sweat it if accidents happen. Just keep a supply of enzyme cleaner handy and sooner or later you will get there!

Potty training can be one of the most frustrating ences for a new puppy owner. There are plenty of b and experts out there who are ready to tell you that if you have even one "accident" in the house, you have failed. Don't believe them and don't let potty accidents ruin your relationship with your dog. Most sensible experts will admit that accidents happen, maybe even daily at first. As long as you're making some form of progress, you will get there sooner or later. A good way of keeping track is to put up a sign on your fridge that says "Days without an accident" and keep track of the number. Perhaps, at first, that number will be zero for a long time. But sooner or later it will become one, then two; and before you know it, you will forget to update it.

2.2 Obedience

An obedient puppy is a well-integrated, happy member of his family. That is why basic obedience should be given top priority over the first few months of your puppy's life with you. It takes time and lots of repetitions, but the good news is that you can teach him the basics of puppy obedience within the first few days! Then it's up to you to repeat and enforce those behaviors in various situations, locations, and at various times.

While discipline is more about the rules of the house, obedience is about specific interactions that you have with your dog in which you ask him to do something and he obeys you. At first, none of this will happen. Lots of dog owners say "oh, my dog doesn't even answer to his name". Your dog doesn't speak English! Unless you teach him, there is no way he can ever answer and obey you. Sure, there are some very rare dogs that figure some basics out

ut that's thanks to their intelligence, not
unication.

k about a puppy who is not at all obedient,
: these complaints in mind:

1. He does not listen to anything I say at all.

2. He does not come when called.

3. He does not respond to any of the position commands such as sit or down.

4. He does not respond to "stay".

5. He does not walk on a leash politely.

These five simple things are often the difference between a puppy which is loved and cared for and one who ends up being sent to the shelter or banished to the yard permanently. We will be taking a look at leash walking in the next chapter in much greater detail, but we can take care of the other four now, as well as show you a few other useful commands.

Paying attention

Before you can get to do any fancy tricks, you need your puppy to pay attention to you. Most of the time, you will set your puppy down in a room and he will immediately start to sniff around, chew on things, play with things, and generally ignore you.

It's a good idea to teach him that whenever you call his name, he should pay attention to you. You have to remember this rule carefully and not mix it up with his recall command, which will be "Name, come!". Just saying his name should get him to look at you, nothing more. For the purpose of this exercise, let's say his name is "Charlie".

You should take Charlie to a distraction-free space for this exercise. The yard is a bad idea, as birds, people, and cats can all pass by and ruin your focus. A room with no toys or anything interesting in it would be ideal.

Getting his attention - exercise

Try sitting down on the floor. When your puppy is looking away, making himself busy, call out "Charlie" in your happiest voice. For many puppies, this might be enough to get him to look at you. If he does, you know what to do – say "yes", offer him treats, praise, and cuddles. Essentially throw him a puppy party.

If the sound of your voice isn't enough to get him to look at you, these extra tricks should help:

- Get lower and closer. Try to be as close to his level as possible and no more than one meter away.

- Call him in a higher tone while making silly waving motions with your hands. Puppies love playtime, so be playful.

- Add a little kiss noise or whistle after his name.

No matter how you get his attention, be sure that it's not by repeating his name a hundred times. Think of his name like a rechargeable phone battery. The more you abuse it, the more you will need to let it charge, so use it sparingly.

As soon as you get his attention in any way, reward him heavily. Then wait until he gets distracted. Call "Charlie" again. At this point, you will have a great indicator of how quickly your puppy learns and how much of a struggle training him will be. The brightest pups will already respond more quickly the second time around, having understood that "Charlie" means treats. Pups which are slower may take a hundred repetitions before they start to get the idea. Most dogs fall somewhere in between.

Your goal is that your pup learns that every time he hears his name, great things happen. His reward can be food, toys, games, or cuddles. Whatever makes him happy will work!

When to practice it

Once he has the basic idea down, call his name whenever you have something good that you're about to give him. Call his name before he has his meals, even if he's already looking at you holding the bowl. Call his name before giving him a delicious treat. Any happy occasion should be a chance to call his name.

When to avoid it

Refrain from ever using his name right before something bad happens unless you want him to run away as soon as he hears it. Most dog owners make the mistake of scolding their dogs for bad behavior by using the phrase "Charlie, no! Bad dog!". Not only is that kind of scolding very ineffective, but it also creates negative connotations with his name that you really don't want to have.

How to advance it

So your puppy has figured it out and every time you say "Charlie" he looks at you and wags his tail expectantly. How can you take this amazing new superpower further? The best thing would be to slowly increase the distance and the level of difficulty.

Call him from one meter, then two, then from across the room. Go outside in the yard, call him from one meter, then two, then across the yard. Get him to look at you while there's someone else in the room with you. Get him to look at you while someone else is playing with a ball, or while there's another dog present. Introduce all new steps very slowly and as soon as one of them becomes too difficult, take a step back. If having another person nearby is too distracting, start with the person being far away. Invent your own ways of making it more difficult, but always give him the chance to learn slowly and set him up to win. You should never give him the chance to fail a command twice in a row!

Sit and down

It may not seem like much now, but knowing sit and down can make a huge difference in how you manage your dog, especially in public situations. It's not about getting him to sit whenever you want it, it's about the fact that while he's sitting and paying attention to you, he's much less likely to go chase whatever passes by.

You can take your dog with you anywhere you want (as long as it's permitted), for example, out for drinks in your local brewery with your friends, if you're certain that you can get him in "down" position, on his blanket, under the table. He can be with you in a crowded queue as long as he's willing to sit patiently by your side. Any time he's in "sit" or "down", it's much less likely that he's going to get up and go.

Sit

Sit is a great command because you can start teaching it right away. Most puppies will get the basic idea within ten minutes. Very smart puppies may start responding to the voice cue by the second day.

Start, as usual, in a distraction-free environment. Have a pocket full of treats, a hungry puppy, and a lot of patience. Take a treat in your hand and hold it tightly between your fingers. Place it close to your puppy's nose.

Now, imagine that the treat and the nose are magnets. You can move one to move the other, but you have to move slowly and keep them close to each other, otherwise the effect wears off. This technique is called "luring".

Slowly lift the treat over his forehead and towards the back of his head. Don't go high up so that he has to jump to get it! Your goal is to get him to move his nose up and his head back. When his head goes backward, his butt will go down. As soon as this happens, let him have the treat and add a few more for good measure!

Repeat this step a few times. When you see that he starts to understand what you want and puts his butt down automatically as soon as you pull out a treat, start saying "Sit" as he is sitting down.

You will have to repeat this exercise hundreds of times over many days before he responds to you saying "sit" without luring him into it. Then a few hundred more before he does it reliably without the treat! Always reward him for obeying you. If you ask him to do it and don't reward him, next time he might not do it.

Down

Use the same principle as for "Sit". When your puppy is sitting, give him a treat. Take another treat in your hand, place it close to his nose, and very very slowly move your hand in a straight line down. When you are halfway down, start also slowly pulling it slightly towards you. Your mission is to get your puppy to bow his head, then stretch out on his belly.

Because this is a harder position than "sit", at first you can reward even intermediate steps, such as following the treat down for a few inches. The first time he moves his front paws forward is also a major milestone. Try doing this on a soft carpeted surface to make it easier on him.

Once he starts to understand what you expect from him, which may take upwards of 20 repetitions, start saying the word "Down" as you are moving the treat downwards. Then repeat the exercise, including the word, as long as it takes for him to get it.

When your puppy begins to anticipate you and goes in to "down" position without needing luring, you can start to give the command to him while standing, from a few steps away, or from across the room. This won't be easy, be prepared and expect it to take many months.

For now, don't expect your dog to stay in this position for a long time. That comes later when you've taught him "stay" and give him both commands together. Remember that "sit" and "down" are just positions, while "sit - stay" and "down – stay" include duration.

Stay

Once your puppy knows "down", you can easily add the command "stay". Catch him in a calm moment, you don't want to teach him this while he's bouncing off the walls! Instead of "luring", this time we have to rely on his intelligence.

When he is in "down" position, calmly but firmly say "Stay", show him your open palm making a "stop" gesture, and reward him. At first, he won't understand what happened – it was barely half a second between the command and the reward.

Next, repeat that but wait one second between saying "Stay" and rewarding him. If that works, count to three next time. Then count to five. If he gets up from his position, calmly say "no", lure him back into "down", and restart from the one second "stay".

Keep extending the time until you get to a count of fifteen. If he gets there successfully, you can start considering moving slightly. First, make a vague gesture of standing up. If he doesn't move, reward him! Slowly build up to you getting up and taking one step back.

Each time your puppy moves, tell him "no" and restart the exercise. Make sure that after that you only give him so little time that he can't mess it up. If it looks like he's getting bored with the exercise, end the session and try again later! Most puppies can only work on "Stay" for a minute or two before getting bored.

Recall

This is the most important command in your arsenal because it could potentially save your puppy's life. It's vitally important that whenever you yell "Charlie, come!" Charlie comes running to you at full speed. Of course, you would substitute "Charlie" for your own pet's name!

The way to begin this is easy. Either use a friend to hold him in place using a harness and leash, or get him in a solid "down" and "stay" position. Walk away from him with your pockets full of treats and your hands full of toys. Yell "Charlie, come!" and jump up and down and throw toys around like you're the most interesting person in the world. If he's being restrained, have your friend release him at that moment. Watch him gallop towards you and enjoy! When he gets to you, throw him a big puppy party. Repeat this exercise many times throughout the day and make sure that at the end of every single "Charlie, Come!", there's a huge reward.

Most owners complain that whenever they yell "Charlie, come!", Charlie either ignores them or runs off in the other direction. There's a very good reason why this happens: Once, when they called their puppy and he didn't come back, they eventually caught him and then scolded him, or smacked him for not coming back sooner. It's understandable, you think a child would understand why he is being punished, so a dog would too, right? Wrong.

He just understood that when you call him, it's because he's about to get scolded, so he has absolutely no reason to come to you. He had no idea why he's being punished, he just knows that when he gets called back, it's bad news.

The absolute most important rule you have to follow is that no matter how bad it gets, even if it takes him an hour to come back, when he eventually does come back, you are not allowed to punish him in any way. On the contrary, you should reward him for coming at all, so that next time he will want to come back even sooner.

If you want to avoid having that problem at all, don't even consider trying to recall him when he's distracted. If you already know he's not coming back because you lost him to a stray squirrel, for example, don't even try it. Go there yourself and bring him back. The more time you spend shouting "Come!" and having him not come, the more you train him that that's an acceptable outcome. Only use this command when you're sure it will be obeyed and always reward it more than you think you should.

Bonus tricks

Any day you teach your puppy something new is a great day for him. While there are thousands of tricks and games he can learn, here are some of the easiest ones that you can work on right away. Perhaps not all of them are useful, but they will all make you and your friends smile.

Shake

A favorite of kids, shake is really easy to teach. Once you have your puppy in a firm "sit-stay", tickle the back of his paw very gently with your fingers. This will cause him to lift it slightly. When he does, say "yes" and reward him. After a few repetitions, take a break. The next time you try him, keep tickling to get his paw to go even higher. When it reaches the right height, gently grab it in your hand and say "shake". Reward him profusely and keep repeating the exercise. They usually learn it in a matter of days!

Spin

Another very easy puppy trick, "spin" simply implies him doing a full 360-degree circle. Not to be confused with "rollover" which is a much more advanced trick. Using the technique of "luring", try to move your puppy around by keeping a treat close to his nose and moving your arm. When he seems confident that following the treat is what you want him to do, simply get him to move in a circle. As he completes the circle, say "spin" and reward. Repeat many times and soon your puppy will spin on command!

Reverse

A very useful trick, reverse is a great way to teach your puppy that he has a rear end. It may seem obvious to you,

but ver)
and oft
takes ti
and th
in such
and p
Then
way t
dowr
Whe
This
and
met

time at the very end of the leash. Both o
and everything in between is perfectly
to worry about.

For puppies that refuse to move
seems like it will last forever,
that is sure to pass sooner
that you put the harne
have fun and play
ground and see if
problem! Try a
fun game,
will take

The
ex

2.?

Sooner or later, you're going to want to take y
out for a walk, and in this case, sooner is better than later. If you're not up to speed with vaccines yet, feel free to take him for walks on isolated streets, through empty fields, through your friend's yards, or anywhere else you can! But take him on a walk for sure.

The general rule is that you would walk a puppy in a harness for a minimum of six months before starting to use a collar. Many people choose to use a harness forever, and that's perfectly fine. Whatever you decide to do, the puppy has to learn how to walk politely before you can even consider putting him in a collar, otherwise, you risk him getting injured.

There are two kinds of puppies. The first kind feels the leash attached to them and plop down on the ground, refusing to move at all. The second kind tears off exploring the second you open the door and spend 100% of their

these situations
normal and nothing

all you need is patience. It
but in reality, it's only a phase
or later. The important thing is
ss on your puppy daily and try to
with him. Toss some treats on the
that will get him moving. If it doesn't, no
gain the next day. If you always make it a
u can be sure that sooner or later your puppy
o his harness and leash.

more common option is that your puppy will want to
plore his surroundings and will be yanking you left and
right every time you're out for a walk. This is also
completely normal. Puppies tend to be very curious and
this is their chance to understand the world. While some
training at this point is essential, don't expect to have a
polite leash-walker until your puppy becomes an adult.

The best thing you can do is to fill your pockets with treats
and toys before going out on your walks. Don't discourage
your puppy from exploring, as this is an important part of
socialization. However, periodically, call him back. Get his
attention with a sharp noise (or his name, if you've done
the exercise from the previous chapter!) And reward him
heavily when he looks at you. This will be much harder to
do while out on the street than it is in the house, so be
prepared to take it slowly and invest in superior quality
treats. Don't bother calling him just as a squirrel is passing
by, it's unreasonable to expect that kind of concentration
from a puppy.

. . .

A regular walk with a young puppy (before six months of age) should follow these steps:

1. Putting on the harness and leash. Try not to take ages with this step as it will agitate your puppy. If the harness is complicated, practice on a toy until you can do it in one or two smooth motions.

2. Waiting until the puppy calms down. If he likes walks, chances are he's going to be jumping up and down like a little maniac at this point. Under no circumstances start the walk until he settles down. Wait as long as it takes.

3. Go out into the street. Look for quiet, remote places. Avoid major distractions and scares such as trucks passing by, dogs barking from behind fences, etc.

4. Let the puppy roam a little. It's better, at this point, to have a slightly longer leash that allows him to sniff around rather than a short one that he will reach the end of in no time. Under no circumstances should you use a retractable leash. They teach puppies to pull!

5. When he gets close to the end of the leash, call him back. For some puppies, this may be after one step; for others, it takes a while. When he comes back, reward him heavily.

6. Take one or two steps with your puppy next to you. Remember the technique called "luring"? Keep treats in your hand and use his nose as a magnet to walk side by side. Reward him after a few steps.

7. Let him roam again. Repeat steps four to seven throughout your walk. Don't let the puppy place himself at the end of the leash and pull like a Husky. The more he does it, the harder it will be to correct.

The other useful trick most puppy parents could benefit

from is an exercise called "You're a tree". With particularly excitable puppies, they may need extra help understanding that the end of the leash is not where you want them to be, and that fun things don't happen there.

The way you set up this information is by freezing and pretending to be a tree every time the leash is pulled tight. When your puppy discovers that the fun has stopped and he can't move forward anymore, he will turn around and look at you. For some puppies, this can take a while, but be resilient. Never ever give in to your puppy pulling, no matter how desperately he is trying to reach something. After a few seconds, if he still isn't looking at you, start taking a few slow steps in the opposite direction to where he is pulling. Our goal is to teach him that as long as the leash is tight, he doesn't get what he wants. When he finally relents and puts some slack in the leash, reward him with an epic puppy party and lots of treats. The grander your rewards are at first, the faster he will learn.

Sometimes, it can seem like a frustrating uphill battle while you're teaching your puppy to walk on a leash. For many months, it's possible that you will only be able to take a step or two in "luring" before he gets distracted. You will look like the world's most indecisive walker, stopping dead every few steps and walking backward one time out of two. You have to persevere. Walking a leash puller can be a nightmare and dangerous for both you and your dog. With perseverance, they can turn into a happy and relaxing experience.

On your walks, there are a few mechanical aspects you should keep in mind. Of course, hot tarmac and delicate puppy paws don't go together, and you should try walking on grass or dirt as much as possible in the summer. It's also a great idea to carry water with you for both yourself and your pup.

Surprisingly, winter comes with its own perils. Ice can be painful to walk on, but puppy pads are decently protected against the cold if you don't over-do it. However, the salt that we humans use on roads in order to prevent icing, is much worse. Walking on salt can be very damaging for young paws, especially if you don't wash them off carefully as soon as you get home. While some people choose to buy dog boots, they're actually awkward to use and not that comfortable for your pup. A much better investment is a tin of good quality pet Paw Balm.

2.4 Socialization

Part of the reason why you want to take your puppy out on regular walks is for exercise. The other part is socialization. You may have heard this word a lot, however, lots of people are confused about what it means because it reminds you of humans "socializing". So it must be allowing your puppy to hang out with other dogs, preferably at the dog park, right?

Not at all. Socialization does include other dogs, but they are only a very small element. When your puppy comes into the world, he's pretty much a blank slate. He needs to spend the next six months of his life figuring out what is "normal" and what is "danger". Socialization is the process by which you teach him to distinguish between these two states.

Lots of literature will give complicated explanations about socialization, imprinting, fear periods, and the various concepts that fall under this category. That's all well and good, but they don't concern you as the owner of a two to six-month-old puppy. You need to know how to handle the practical side of things simply and with confidence.

The most important socialization effort you need to make for your puppy is to consider all of the possible things that your adult dog may run into throughout his whole life. Some of these are easy to guess: cars, large animals, small animals, storms, umbrellas, masks, children, fences. Write down a list of the most important ones. Others may depend on your specific living conditions: Do you garden? Do you have strange tools and machinery in the garage? Do you have funny people over all the time? Do you foster pets? Do you have farm animals? Do you go to a lot of outdoor concerts? Do you take the bus or train a lot?

For the first six months of your puppy's life with you, the most important thing you can possibly do is take him from place to place, from event to event, and from person to person, and show him that all of these things fall under "normal" and not "danger".

It's called a "socialization window" because, like a real window, it closes. Once your pup is about eight months old, anything he's never seen and doesn't know how to handle can and will be treated as "danger". To some dogs, this may mean being nervous, shy, or frightened. To others, it might be a call to arms.

Most puppy owners socialize badly in two major ways. One common version is that of the excessively confident puppy parent which simply throws her dog in a dog park and hopes for the best. This doesn't actually help with socializing because once your puppy has met a couple of dogs and got the idea, anything beyond that isn't "socializing" anymore. It can also foster bad play habits or a fear of other dogs if they suffer a traumatic experience while at the park. You have little control and that's not ideal.

The other version is that of the overly-protective parent. They try to "socialize" their puppy while holding him in their arms the entire time. Whenever the puppy gets frightened or shy, they pick them up and walk away. Whenever the puppy growls, they pick them up and walk away. The problem with this kind of attitude is that it reinforces your dog's belief that something is "dangerous". You picked him up, therefore he was right – it was a dangerous situation. Phew.

Unless you're actually in a dangerous situation, that can have serious consequences. You don't want to teach your dog to be afraid every time a car passes by, a dog sniffs her, or another puppy play-growls. In most situations, it's better to be close to your puppy, but allow her to explore life naturally and normally without stressing her out. Calmly carry on with what you're doing and she will pick up the cues and stay calm too.

When socializing, try to hit these major points, but be sure to add your own:

- Family members, neighbors, friends, and their pets

- Strangers around town and their dogs

- Cars, bikes, trucks, etc., passing by

- Being in the car, going for a drive

- Being on public transport

- Funny noises like people dragging things on the ground or loud engines

- Sunglasses, hoods, hats, umbrellas, masks

- People and dogs running or playing sports

- People having a loud argument

- Strange smells like gas stations or food markets

- Climbing into objects such as boxes, on top of objects such as benches, going around objects such as concrete posts, going through tunnels or narrow passageways

- Climbing stairs

- Walking on metal grates, concrete, leaves, sand, grass

- Having a leash, harness, and collar put on daily

- Being touched, being handled, going to the vet, going to the groomer

- Being brushed and washed

- Any time anyone says "My dog is scared of" make a note and prevent the same thing happening to your dog!

This socialization window is a strange and fun period for both owner and puppy. You should find yourself often going out of your way to meet strangers, investigate strange noises, and do strange things. You will often find yourself giving your dog treats while other people are talking to you or even petting him. You should also allow strange people to give him treats (which you supply). The good news is that most people love puppies and this will be a lot easier than it sounds.

What happens if your puppy has a negative experience during his socialization window? This is something we want to avoid at all costs. A simple negative experience such as a child pulling his tail painfully while you're distracted for one second can turn into a lifelong habit of running from, or worse, attacking children. You should exert control at all times so that interaction with new things happens under your terms. If something unwanted happens, it will be your job to focus on replacing that one negative experience with a hundred good ones.

2.5 Grooming

It may seem strange, but the first part of learning how to groom your puppy actually coincides with part of his socialization! It's important to let him know that being touched is a normal part of being a puppy. This includes sensitive areas such as paws, tail, belly, mouth, and ears. You also have to introduce water, the tub, the brush, and the nail clippers slowly. You won't be able to get much grooming done before this step!

Grooming needs change from dog to dog, but there are a few unavoidable steps for all dog owners. The major ones are fur care, nail care, and oral hygiene. Getting your puppy accustomed to being groomed is an essential part of your daily activities.

Oral hygiene

It's a good idea to start practicing this early and frequently because it can be a sensitive moment for many dogs. Most dogs won't automatically allow you to touch their face, let alone open their mouth, but it's your job as a caring parent to slowly show your puppy that there's nothing to be scared of.

On the first day, this would probably only be light touches close to the face followed by rewards. If it seems your puppy is particularly easygoing, touching the face directly and rewarding is still fine.

By the end of the first week, you should build up to putting your hands around the puppy's snout for a second, gently and without any pressure, and rewarding heavily when he lets you do it.

By the end of two weeks, you want to be able to lift his lips gently without causing him any stress and without putting much pressure on his lips. This is a good time to take a look at his baby teeth and keep an eye on any permanent teeth that might be coming along!

By the end of the first month, you should be able to use a finger brush specifically designed for brushing puppy teeth to clean his teeth for a few seconds. Toothpaste is not as important to them as it is to us, and the simple mechanical process of brushing should be more than enough. Don't add any unnecessary discomfort at this point by doing it for more than a few seconds at a time or by adding strange tastes to the equation.

Once your puppy is comfortable with having his teeth brushed, you can fall into a regular rhythm of brushing depending on his needs. This should, ideally, happen every few days.

Nail cutting

Nail cutting can be very tricky and many pet owners choose to have their pet's nails cut professionally. It doesn't have to be frightening however. Most of the time, cutting nails at home is less stressful and traumatic for your dog. All you need is a good quality dog nail clipper – accept no substitute! Absolutely do not use human clippers for this job.

Your goal at first will be to touch your puppy's paws daily and get him comfortable with that. Reward him after every time you touch his paws so that he makes a positive, happy association with that gesture. Do it during happy, playful moments and don't extend the time or the level of pressure until he's comfortable.

When touching his paws becomes a normal, day-to-day activity, try picking him up and holding his paws in your hands for a few seconds. Reward him for any increase in tolerance and don't overdo it. When you can gently squeeze a paw for a few seconds with no problem, start touching the nail clippers to your puppy's nails. If he seems startled by the sensation, that's perfectly normal. Take a step back and ease him into it.

If he's fine with it, you can start by clipping just the very tips of his nails. If you're lucky and have a white nailed pup, you should be able to see that inside his white nail there's a pink center called a "quick". Ideally, you should cut in such a way that you never risk touching this pink area, as that would be extremely painful for your pup. If it does happen, be sure to put some styptic powder on the nail, and don't try to clip his nails again for a while.

If your puppy has black nails, it will be harder to tell and you have to be even more careful. Special nail clippers with infrared sensors exist, or you can clip off thin slices until you start to see a white center to the nail. Look up images online for clipping black dog nails and you will have a good reference point.

Fur care

When it comes to caring for your puppy's fur, you will need to research what specific needs his breed has. Each type of brush is better suited to certain types of fur, so make sure you get the right ones. Brushing your puppy should start off in the same way as everything else: first, get him used to the motions and tools involved. Pet him frequently and try using a microfiber cloth of glove before moving on to a brush. Since brushing is pleasant, most puppies take to it quickly.

Bathing, on the other hand, is where most puppies get hung up. If you rush this process, you risk having a dog that is afraid of the bathtub for life, so be careful. Before washing your pup, get him accustomed to all of the individual elements of bath time separately: the empty tub, the smell of the soap, the feeling of the towel, running water near him, running water on him. Only when he seems comfortable with all of these should you put them together into one single event. Try to keep baths as quick and simple as possible, at first, and don't be ashamed of keeping treats and chews by the tub to occasionally encourage him.

You should take care to buy a bottle of all-natural dog shampoo that is suitable for your individual dog's skin and coat. Try to read the ingredients list and make an investment in a natural, hypoallergenic brand. You won't be using large quantities of it, so you might as well spring for the superior shampoo.

Thoroughly rinse your pet's fur and if you repeat the shampoo (according to the instructions on the bottle), be sure to rinse well the second time around too. When drying your dog, it's better to use towels and let him shake it off whenever it's warm enough. If you use a hairdryer, it has to be either designed specifically for dogs or set on a "cool air" setting. Your puppy will also know what to do: one good shake will get most of the water out of his fur and onto your walls, so hang out in the bathroom for a little bit.

No matter what you do, chances are you're going to get

dog hair around the house and on your clothes. Breeds with shorter hair tend to shed more than breeds with long hair, but all dogs shed to some extent. Regular brushing with the right brush and bathing help with this problem to some extent, however, they don't cure it completely. It may be better to simply be prepared and buy a few rolls of sticky hair-removing tape for your clothing and couch.

Other puppy care tips

It's a good idea to keep a close eye on your puppy's eyes, nose, and ears at all times. Look inside the ears and if needed, clean them with a soft cotton cloth every now and then. Take note of any particular discharge coming from these areas and ask your veterinarian if you have any doubts or concerns.

When it comes to outerwear, use your judgment. Dogs that are well-suited for cooler climates and have nice thick fur don't need jackets and are only going to suffer while wearing them. Labradors are sturdy and waterproof and will do just fine without clothing; however, if you're living somewhere in colder climate, one may be needed.

2.6 Nutrition

Your puppy is going to spend the first year of his life converting whatever food you give him into strong muscles and bones. The quality and quantity of the food you provide for him in this period are absolutely essential. While not all budgets are created equal, you're not really saving money if you're going to spend it all on veterinary bills in the near future.

When planning his diet, take into consideration that he will only need a good quality dry food, treats and rewards, chewy things, and freshwater. Dogs don't need wet food the way cats do, so it's better to take that money and invest it in premium quality kibble. Some very good brands can be found online and delivered to your doorstep.

When you first get your puppy, they will have been eating a specific brand of food at the breeder or shelter. Find out what that brand is and get a bag since you can't abruptly switch over to a new food. A newly-adopted puppy has plenty of frightening things to worry about and doesn't need the added problem of indigestion. Start mixing in your brand of choice after a few days, slowly increasing the quantity until his diet is made up entirely of what you intend to feed him until he becomes an adult.

You should feed puppies puppy-specific food until they are fully grown, however, breed specific food is not necessary and often it's less nutritious than other varieties. You can recognize good quality dog food by learning to read labels. Don't fall for packaging that claims it's "healthy", "organic", "natural", etc. Those words don't mean anything. All you need to know is in the ingredients list.

Whatever food you pick should absolutely NOT have:

- corn and wheat gluten

- artificial coloring or flavors

- meat and grain meals and by-products

- anything other than meat as a first ingredient

Ideally, the ingredients list should contain:

- real meat as a first ingredient

- named animals and organs, not just generic "meat product"

- rice or peas as the carbohydrate

- a high protein content (ideally over 30%)

Veterinarians often recommend a specific brand, but you don't necessarily have to take that as a definitive answer. Most of the time, they are sponsored by that brand. Most dog food bags will come with instructions on serving quantities depending on your puppy's breed, age, and weight; however, these are more often than not exaggerated. A much better indicator of how much your puppy needs to eat is checking out breeder websites and each breed's caloric requirements.

Puppies should ideally be fed two to three times a day. You can expect them to need a bathroom break within fifteen minutes after each feeding if everything is going well. Under no circumstances should you leave food out for your puppy all the time. Meal times and quantities should be fixed, and the bowl should be emptied within a few minutes. If your puppy is leaving food in the bowl, then there is something wrong. Either he doesn't like the food, he is feeling sick, or you are overfeeding.

The best way to know whether you're giving your puppy the right amount of food is to examine him. Look at a short haired breed or touch a long haired one to see if you can feel his ribs. You're supposed to be able to feel them with your fingers, but not see them. Your puppy is going to look chubby, but as he grows into an adolescent dog, he should have a visible waistline. He should maintain this waistline throughout his life. A dog that is straight all the way from his shoulders to his pelvis is overweight.

It's very easy to lose track of how much we are feeding our puppies, especially during their first few months of life because they get so many rewards and treats. You have to always take care to feed less when you treat more and should even consider using all of his kibble allocation for the day as treats and rewards. Hand-feeding during training sessions is a wonderful bonding experience between you and your pup. At any rate, don't think that you can get away with giving him treats on top of his regular meals.

Having fresh clean water available at all times is of the utmost importance. Puppies get very easily dehydrated, especially in the summer, while playing and running around. Early signs of puppy dehydration are dry and sticky gums and tongue. In a normal state, his gums and tongue should be wet. Another easy way to tell he's dehydrated is if the skin on his back and shoulders don't spring right back after being gently pulled up.

It's fine to remove the water bowl after dinner however, and set it back down before breakfast. If we drink a large amount of water before going to bed, we need to get up at night. It's the same for our puppy and we want him to sleep through the night as soon as possible.

If your puppy is eating a complete and balanced diet, you have no reason to worry about supplements. Adding vitamins and minerals can actually upset the balance in his body and be harmful to his growth. Supplements are not something you should ever consider without a specific recommendation from your vet.

3

PREVENTING AND CORRECTING PROBLEMS

Let's face it, puppies can be awful at times. They grow up to become amazing, wonderful dogs; however, when they're young, they can feel like a complete disaster. It sometimes seems like they chew everything they see, chase everything they see, and pee on everything they see. There's no such thing as a trouble-free puppy. Bringing a dog into your life and home is a massive responsibility and that decision should not be taken lightly.

In an ideal world, when we bring a puppy home, we will be able to remember all of the instructions we ever read, we will never make a mistake, and our puppy will be perfect. In the real world, however, that never happens. Real life gets in the way of even the most well-meaning of training schedules. Mistakes happen, family members have conflicting ideas of what "educated" means, and plans go out the window.

Puppies who are misbehaving are never doing it on purpose. They aren't capable of evil, that's one of the reasons why we love them. Every dog does every single action fully convinced that he's doing the right thing. Even when a frightened dog bites a person, they're just doing what they learned was right: defending themselves. There's absolutely no cause to ever get angry at a dog and no excuse for letting them suffer when we could help them understand the world.

Since we are the ones to blame for their mistakes, it's only fair that we should know how to set things right when they go wrong. Prevention is ideal, but even if the damage is already done, there is always a way to make things better for both you and your dog.

3.1 Redirecting, Reinforcing, Exercising

The three most important techniques you need to know as a pet parent are redirecting, reinforcing, and the power of exercise. If you understand the concept of these, you can adapt them to any situation and any problem you may be having with your puppy.

Redirecting

Many first-time puppy owners don't realize that scolding your puppy almost never works. It's very rare that they will actually understand what they are being scolded for. Even if they do, chances are they will develop negative associations with you as well as with that situation.

So what are you supposed to do when you catch your puppy in the act of doing something bad? The best option possible is to calmly, but firmly remove him from the problem and redirect him onto the appropriate version of that activity. Then you reward him for doing the right thing.

If you catch him chewing slippers, you take away the slipper calmly and replace it with a delicious chew bone. You are redirecting him to the appropriate toy. If he would rather chew slippers, then you're not making his chew bones appealing enough – feel free to cheat and dip them in sodium-free chicken broth, rub them all over with a slice of hot-dog, or any other trick you can think of that will make them smell appealing to your dog.

If you catch him about to pee on the carpet, you calmly take him outside and redirect him to the appropriate potty area. When he does use it, reward him. If he's pulling desperately on the leash to get to a squirrel, back away a good distance and redirect him onto some amazing toys and treats that are even more interesting than the squirrel.

Redirecting can be a powerful tool and it can be used in almost any situation. It should be your automatic answer whenever your dog is doing something he shouldn't be doing. That is why you should always keep his treats, toys, and chews within reach and even take some with you on walks.

Reinforcing

Unlike redirecting, which is our automatic answer whenever our puppy does something bad, reinforcing is our automatic answer whenever he does something good. It's not enough to keep telling him what not to do – you can't expect him to read a book or play chess. You need to also give him options of what to do and express your approval when he does them.

Reinforcing is what we've been doing every single time we rewarded our puppy's good behavior. He does something, we are happy about it, we reward him, and that behavior is reinforced as being good behavior. Reinforcing doesn't happen overnight and one treat doesn't make an obedient puppy. But each time he does something and it has a positive outcome, he's a little more likely to do that same thing again.

You already know about reinforcing your puppy when he goes potty in the correct place, or when he performs "sit" or "down" for you. But there are hundreds of situations throughout a normal day in which you can take advantage of what your puppy is naturally doing in order to reinforce it. Think about what you would ideally want your dog to be like and work towards constructing that kind of behavior.

Some of the best things to reinforce by rewarding:

- Whenever he goes calmly and happily to nap on his bed. Yes, even if it disturbs him.

- Whenever he meets somebody new and approaches them confidently but calmly.

- Whenever he sits close to you. Whenever he follows you and pays attention to you.

- Whenever he brings you something. This is important if you ever want to teach him to play fetch.

- Whenever he doesn't react badly to a scary situation, such as a loud noise.

- Whenever he is chewing on his own toys.

- Whenever he refrains from chasing the cat.

There are hundreds of other situations, depending on what

your home life looks like. Find the ones that are important to you and reinforce positive behavior.

While reinforcing can be a great thing, you also have to be very careful with it. It's easy to accidentally reinforce bad behaviors by allowing them to be rewarded. For example, every time your dog jumps on you and you give him a cuddle, you are reinforcing him jumping on people. Think about how that may feel to strangers, children, or the elderly. Be very careful what behavior you choose to reinforce.

Exercising

The most important tool in your arsenal for bad behavior prevention is exercise. It holds true that a tired puppy is a happy puppy, but even more so that a tired puppy doesn't have the energy to get into trouble. Labradors, in particular, tend to have a lot of energy, but so do many other dogs.

Puppies have even more energy than their adult counterparts, so it stands to reason that the only way you can ensure a few hours of peace and quiet is by providing them with vigorous exercise. The fun thing about puppies is that their exercise requirements take three forms, and all three of these forms have to be fulfilled: physical, mental, and social.

Letting a puppy run around in a large yard may give him a chance to stretch his legs, but won't actually do much in the way of keeping him calm and satisfied because there are no mental or social elements to that exercise. Similarly, doing lots of obedience sessions in a day may be exhausting, but he will still need a chance to run and stretch his legs.

The best day for a puppy includes a nice long walk, which is physically tiring but also gives you a chance to practice obedience and to socialize. Playing with you at home is also important. Tug of war is always a favorite game for puppies as it releases a lot of tension and is quite tiring. Playing fetch is great, but won't substitute for walks and interaction as it isn't very mentally stimulating.

You should include short training sessions, as well as the chance to play with other people or animals. On a day that includes all of these activities, you can be pretty sure that your puppy won't get bored and get into mischief.

It's important to keep in mind, however, that puppies are still growing. Their muscles and bones aren't fully developed, and some types of exercise can create serious problems. Most notably, jumping is not something that you should encourage until after your puppy has stopped growing. Walks and tug of war are generally safe for all breeds.

The other important thing to remember is that getting two dogs and hoping they will play with each other isn't going to get you off the hook when it comes to exercise. They might, but it won't fulfill their needs at all. Puppies need regular interaction with humans and lots of dogs to be happy, as well as walks and obedience training. Getting two puppies will be double the responsibility and take twice as much effort to educate, so don't rush into that decision.

3.2 Unwanted biting and chewing

We've spoken a little bit about unwanted chewing in our section on redirection, but we need to take a closer look at this very common puppy problem. When you get your puppy, most likely he will have two rows of needle-sharp tiny teeth. Their teeth are insanely sharp to make up for the fact that they don't have as much strength in their jaw.

Most puppies are going to use their teeth in two major ways: to chew things and to chew your hands. This behavior is perfectly normal, but you do have to keep it under control. It's your job to make sure that the objects being chewed are the right ones and that his play-biting doesn't get out of hand.

When it comes to chewing, you should invest in a variety of puppy-appropriate chew toys to keep his mouth busy, particularly during that terrible teething stage in which it seems that their mouth is never empty. Puppies would rather chew on softer objects at first, like your slippers or the pillow, and it's hard to get them to let go. Things that smell like you are going to be particularly interesting.

If you want to keep up with his curious mouth, you can't expect to just throw toys on the ground and let him have at them. That may work for some pups, but not for most. Here's a list of tricks that you can use to make chew toys more appealing:

- Offer a variety of textures from soft to durable

- Dunk them in sodium-free chicken broth

- Store them in his kibble bag

- Rub them with delicious treats

- Fill them with food – especially the Kong

- Keep them in your pocket for a while

- Use them as toys if they are soft enough. Toss them, tug them, make them move.

The more he chews on his own toys, the more the habit

gets reinforced, the more he is likely to do it again. Find a way to get the ball rolling.

It's not a good idea to provide puppies with stuffed toys. While stuffed animals are cute for us, they will become just another chew toy to the puppy. Tearing up and destroying a stuffed animal is actually very pleasant, so once they get a taste for it, you can expect them to do the same to your pillows. It's also not a good idea to use squeaky toys. Most of the time these contain small parts that could be easily swallowed. Shop around and look at your options before making a decision.

Kong puppy toys are very popular. They are rubbery cones which are hollow on the inside, allowing you to stuff food and treats in there. Puppies have to work out how to get the food out by chewing, rolling, dropping, and licking the toy. These toys are an amazing resource because they can keep your puppy occupied for a long time. Many parents feed their puppies entirely from Kong toys for the first few months in order to provide extra mental stimulation and exercise. You can fill them with anything, including their regular kibble, and you can even pop them in the freezer for a cool treat that will soothe the aching gums of a teething pup.

Play biting is a whole other matter. While chewing is a soothing, calming activity, play biting is exciting and fun for your puppy. All puppies are mouthy, and all puppies grow out of it – with the right care.

In most cases, stopping puppy biting is a two-step process. The first step is making it clear that you don't like it, and the second step is offering an alternative. When puppies play with each other and things get a little too rough, they yelp. That usually gets everyone to stop what they are doing. Similarly, when your puppy gets too rough on your hands, giving out a loud "ouch" should be enough to make them stop for a second.

Have either a tug toy or treats handy at all times and redirect mouthy behavior into obedience training or a game of tug. Continue to redirect every time it happens and reward your puppy for choosing to chew on his toys or play tug instead of attacking your hands.

Some puppies have a stronger prey drive than others. That's the impulse that makes them want to attack anything that moves and keep attacking it until it stops moving. Luckily, Labradors are intelligent breeds smart enough to learn when to stop.

The rule is that every time your puppy bites your hands too hard – it's up to you to decide how much is acceptable, "gentle" biting and what crosses over the line – you have to pick him up and put him in a one-minute time-out. This can be either in a room, a playpen, or a crate. It's possible that he will complain and bark, in which case you can't let him out until he settles down – you don't want to reinforce barking and whining.

This time-out rule has to be strict and happen every time, otherwise, it won't mean anything to your puppy. When you let him out, propose a game of tug of war. If he still insists on going after your feet or hands, put him in time-out again. The reason why time-out is very important for puppies with high prey drive is that they get so excited they simply can't be reasoned with anymore. A brief time-out will help calm them down.

There are signs that will let you know if your puppy is one of the highly excitable, high-prey drive pups that benefit from time-outs. Usually, they won't even flinch no matter how loudly you yell "ouch". Sometimes they may even get more riled up and go after your hands and feet even more. Usually, once they start attacking your feet, it becomes impossible to distract them even with treats or toys. If you have a puppy who is willing to ignore a delicious treat, then it's clear that he's overexcited and needs a little timeout.

3.3 Chasing

The history of our beloved pets is quite interesting. Their jobs ranged from protector to hunter to loving companion, and they were bred to do those jobs to perfection. They all come from the same common ancestor however, and that ancestor is a hunter.

When we talk about a specific breed's prey drive, we talk about the natural instinct that makes that breed want to catch a moving object and the tenacity with which they will pursue it. Prey drive is what makes a dog jump up and chase a ball, cat, or bird. Prey drive is also what makes them nibble at your heels when they're overexcited and you're moving.

A dog with low prey drive may not feel like getting up from his comfortable spot in the sun just to chase a ball. He is also a lot less likely to be mad at passing birds, chase other pets around the house, or get excited as soon as you pick up a toy. It's potentially a great thing, depending on what you want from your dog.

A dog with high prey drive is going to become an expert at fetching the ball and catching a Frisbee in the air. He is well suited for lots of games, but he's also very likely to annoy other pets, fixate on squirrels and birds, and kill any small animals in his part. This type of dog isn't even recommended for households that have small pets like parrots or guinea pigs; however, they can be amazing sports companions.

No matter what kind of dog you end up with, there are situations in which you don't want him to chase everything that moves. It's always hard to keep a balance between discouraging unwanted chasing but not discouraging participation in chasing games. Scolding or punishing a dog for chasing can easily end up suppressing his prey drive; and if he's sensitive, that may mean he will never play ball with you. It doesn't sound like a tragedy, but handling an energetic dog without the benefit of fetch, Frisbee, tug of war, or lure chasing is an absolute nightmare.

Most commonly, people complain about unwanted chasing in two major situations: during walks and at home with other pets. There are plenty of other possible instances where it might happen, but the same solutions would apply. Keep in mind, however, that to some extent all puppies chase and there's no stopping them completely. Nor should you, it is a normal healthy instinct of any dog. Training them not to chase pigeons isn't an excuse for letting them off the leash near a busy street. There are some stimuli that even the most well-behaved dog won't be able to resist. Leashes are there for a reason.

When you're out with your dog, potential chase hazards include birds, cats, other dogs, squirrels, leaves, and anything else that moves. If you're unlucky, small children running around could easily fall under this category.

The trick is not to throw your dog in the deep end of the pool all of a sudden. You have to teach him to resist temptation slowly. Ideally, practice his leash walking and keeping his attention on you for a long time on empty streets with no distractions. Then, repeat those same exercises within view of moving objects, but not closer. Then, when your puppy is comfortable paying attention to you while there are kids running or bicycles in sight, move a little closer to them. As soon as he starts to give in to that impulse to chase, step back a few meters to where he has more control and practice again. Keep his attention on you with treats and toys and make slow progress towards your target.

It will take months of keeping him attentive within sight of chase triggers before you can go near them. This is not a fast process. Your goal is to be able to walk with your dog through a crowded street without him tugging towards other dogs, kids, or birds; but it can take some time to build up to that. The self-control exercise we will be discussing shortly also helps with this.

When it comes to at-home shenanigans, it may be a little harder to keep things in hand. You don't always have a handy leash to pull him back from distractions and he's not always paying attention to you. So when the cat or a bike or the postman pass by, it's fair game. This can be a serious problem, particularly for the other pets in your household. You need to help your puppy practice self-restraint, as well as teach him the "leave it" command. The following exercise does both and is very important. You should never underestimate the power of self-restraint for a dog.

Leave it

Do you remember the reward and punishment exercise from the beginning of this book? If not, now is a good time to check it out and start working on it because it is the basis of this exercise.

If you have done your homework, then by now you should

be able to hold a treat in your fist and have your puppy leave it alone and wait patiently for you to open it and give it to him. It's time to build on that and work up to one of the most amazing commands you can ever teach your dog, which is "leave it".

Get down on the floor. Put a treat in your hand and close your fist over it. Make sure your puppy knows it's there. Put your closed fist in front of him. He should know the trick by now and wait patiently.

Instead of saying "Yes" and letting him have the treat, open your fist slowly. As soon as he makes a move for the treat, close it again. When he stops, open it slowly again. It should take a few tries before you get to open your fist all the way with your puppy still waiting patiently. Don't keep him waiting for long! As soon as he doesn't immediately lunge for the treat, say "Yes" and reward him heavily.

Repeat this many times and once it looks like he gets the idea, as you open your fist, add the command "leave it". Slowly, over many days, increase the time you take before saying "yes" to a few seconds. If you say "leave it" and the puppy lunges for the treat, close your fist, calmly say "no", and try again. If he seems frustrated, take a break and next time shorten the wait times.

Keep repeating this until he knows what you expect from him. Then, after saying "leave it", very slowly place the treat on the ground. Give him half a second of waiting time and say "yes", at which point he should lunge for it. Slowly increase the duration of the exercise. Be sure to do this in short sessions over many days!

When your puppy is comfortable leaving the treat on the ground for a few seconds, and he has more or less under-stood the concept of "leave it", the real fun begins. Start by gently rolling the treat on the ground in front of him while he waits for it. Progress to flicking it a few centimeters away from him. Progress to tossing it across the room. Work your way up, slowly as always, to being able to say "leave it" and tossing the treat across the room from standing height. Be sure to take your time to make sure every single step is nailed down before you move on to the next one. If your puppy gets up to chase the treat, you have failed by moving too fast. Next time, be sure to make it so easy for him that he can't possibly make a mistake again. Don't ever give him the chance to get it wrong twice in a row.

Once you get good at the "leave it" game, practice it outside. Try it with a ball or tug toy. Bring treats with you wherever you go and work on "leave it" whenever you can: on the street, in queues, at restaurants. The more you do it, the better your chances that it will sink in. Soon, you will be able to drop a chicken leg in the kitchen, shout "leave it", and pick it back up without your dog snatching it! That kind of self-control takes a long time and a lot of practice.

The great thing about this exercise is that once "leave it" becomes a part of your puppy's vocabulary, you can use it to stop him chasing the cat, birds, or anything else. Remember to work your way up to the harder ones slowly and reward him a great deal every time he obeys you. "Leave it" can be a lifesaving tool that prevents your dog from eating a dropped pill, a mushroom in the woods, or a decaying corpse. It can prevent him from dashing across the road to chase a cat. It can save his life in so many ways that it's fully worth the time and effort.

3.4 Aggression and reading body language

When people think of "aggression" in relation to dogs, they often imagine that an "aggressive" dog is a bad dog. There is a great difference between aggression in general and unwanted aggression, but they have one thing in common: in neither case is the dog to blame.

Dogs can become aggressive for many reasons. It often happens to dogs that were deprived of proper socialization in their youth, or dogs who experienced a traumatic event and now react aggressively because they are afraid. An adult dog that has a serious unwanted aggression problem is going to need the help of a professional behaviorist, and you should seek their guidance and counsel before trying anything by yourself.

All puppies have a certain level of aggression. It's a natural trait in all animals and is a good and healthy element of their personality. Aggression is what makes him play tug of war with you or guard the house for you. It may save his life in a dangerous situation. There's nothing wrong with a normal amount of well-controlled aggression. However, we want to prevent those seeds from sprouting into full-blown trees of unwanted aggression problems.

The first step in preventing unwanted aggression is being able to identify it. Lots of websites and books like to give out helpful charts or photos showing various dog positions and telling you what emotion each position means. You need to understand one thing right now: none of that is true. While some gestures and motions can sometimes indicate certain emotions, there is absolutely no guarantee that that's the case. Each dog is different. Some breeds trick you on purpose. You can never rely on body language in a potentially dangerous situation with an unknown dog. You have been warned.

Often you will be told that a dog wagging his tail is

friendly. This terrible advice is usually given to children and puts them in the most danger. The reality is that almost all dogs wag their tails when they are friendly, but some will also do it when they are agitated, excited, or angry. Brave harrier breeds like terriers can often get so excited about chasing and killing something that they will wag their tails. That's not something you should bet your safety on.

A dog that has his tail between his legs is usually nervous or frightened, that is true. However, fear in dogs can manifest in many ways. They may freeze, they may feel better if you approach them and comfort them, or they may decide to defend themselves. The great majority of cases of unwanted aggression towards humans stem from fear, so a tail between the legs on an unknown dog should be a warning sign.

We also always imagine that a dog who is about to attack you will be growling, snarling, snapping, and have the hair raised on the back of their heads. For many dogs that is not the case. Infamously, Rottweilers can look perfectly calm until the very last second. However, if they do have raised hairs going down their back, then you can be sure it's trouble.

The point is that the only reliable body language you can be sure to recognize, is the one that belongs to your individual puppy, by observing him over many months and knowing how he reacts in different situations. Only experience can help you understand what your puppy is saying with his body.

When it comes to puppies, "unwanted aggression" can take many shapes, but you will know it when you see it. Here are some very common signs that you might have an unusually aggressive pup:

- He growls to defend his toys or food

- He goes for your hands and feet when he's excited

- He doesn't quit no matter what treats you offer

- He fixates on certain situations which always trigger him

- He freezes and stares at you when you reach for his bowl or blanket

- He nips at you when you try to touch him or wake him up

These situations are all unnerving, especially if they happen repeatedly. Many puppy owners have lost their temper because they experienced one or all of these. It's crucial that you don't respond to aggressive behavior with more aggressive behavior, as that can have wild and unexpected consequences.

The first thing you should do is check in with your veterinarian and make sure that everything is fine. A lot of puppies who are sick or in pain will react aggressively, so if he suddenly starts to show this kind of behavior, look out for any other symptoms of illness. If you've ruled that out, here are some other things you can do:

- Redirect him. Just like in our explanation on redirection, you will need to have some other outlet on hand for him to vent his aggression. It's a good idea, especially if you have excitable puppies, to stash tug ropes all over the house. That way, whenever he wants to take it out on you, he can take it out on a rope instead.

- Put him in time-out. If there's no stopping him, a short time-out to cool off is the only thing you can do. Don't make these time-outs long, they aren't an excuse for you to go away and ignore your puppy for hours. A few minutes tops should do it, then if he comes out just as excited, put him back for a few minutes more. Be sure to place him in time-out calmly and gently.

- Keep him in a harness and leash, even around the house, during moments which you know will trigger him. If he goes crazy every time your kids get home from school, for example, that would be a great time to keep him in check using a leash. Take it off again when the moment passes.

These are immediate responses that you can use in case of trouble, however, there are many more things that you can do in order to prevent this kind of trouble from showing up at all. First on your list should be providing adequate exercise and mental stimulation for your puppy. A tired puppy is a happy puppy. Don't give him the chance to have spare energy to burn at the end of the day because it's very likely that he will burn it in unfortunate ways.

Sometimes, as is the case for small children, being excessively tired can also cause puppies to be grumpy and angry. You may notice, for example, that when you get home from a very long walk, he gets agitated and starts biting your heels as soon as you reach the door. He may have a bout of inexplicable, crazy running in the yard or through the rooms. These are classic signs of a tired pup. Thankfully, the very simple and effective cure for that is to put him in his crate for a nap. When they get that tired, you can expect them to sleep it off for at least an hour or two!

Teaching your pup basic obedience commands either by yourself or by going to an educator can be invaluable. It's not just about having the ability to say "sit" and have your pup sit. That may work and it may interrupt his aggressive behavior. But more importantly, it creates a bond between the two of you that will improve your understanding of each other.

84

Similarly, spending time playing and having fun with your pup will also strengthen that bond. The more he plays with you – tug, fetch, hide and seek – the more he will understand you and what your rules and limits are. You can initiate play and stop it whenever it gets too rough or you get tired. You can show him that you're a fun person to be around as long as he plays nicely. By simply playing, you will be teaching him more than you can imagine.

Another very important effort in preventing unwanted aggression in adult dogs is proper socialization as puppies. We've spoken about socialization previously, but the specific area of it that helps prevent aggression problems is intraspecies socialization. That means interacting from an early age with other dogs. The reason why this is important is that dogs have ways of transmitting messages to each other that we can't even fathom. It's not just a growl or body language, it's scent and chemical reactions as well.

When a puppy interacts with an adult dog, for example, the adult dog will automatically take a dominant position in their relationship. He will allow the puppy to play and even play-bite, but if it gets out of hand, the adult dog can easily stop him and make it very clear why. Whereas you can stop the puppy, but will always struggle to explain the "why" to him. When playing with each other, puppies have their own system. Even though to us it looks like a painful mess of teeth and claws, they are following instinctive rules which you wouldn't be able to impose. When one puppy bites too hard, the other emits a piercing squeak and leaves the game. Puppies that insist on biting too hard or playing too rough eventually get ostracized and have nobody to play with, so they quickly learn to stay within the limits.

In order to reap the benefits of this kind of socialization, you need to get it done in the right context. A dog park is your worst nightmare because you have no control over who goes in it and what goes on there. A much better option would be a group puppy training class. You should also organize play dates with other friendly puppies or adult dogs, as well as attend dog-friendly events or parties. Great socialization sessions should last long enough for the dogs to play to their satisfaction, but not so long that they grow tired and grumpy. Depending on your dog, this can mean anything from ten minutes to two hours.

While passing other dogs in the street and greeting them is always a fun puppy activity, that won't count much towards preventing aggressive behavior since there just isn't enough time for them to interact and communicate.

While we're on the topic of meeting other dogs on the street, let's talk about puppies who have excessive aggressive reactions towards other dogs while on a leash. To some extent, it's normal that not all dogs will get along with all other dogs. Some puppies are just sweet and good-natured and will make friends easily, and pet owners are often deluded into thinking that this would, or should, be the case for all dogs. It's actually far more common that dogs will not always make friends, especially within the same gender, and almost never in the case of unneutered males. We need to put our expectations aside and instead settle for them tolerating or ignoring other dogs.

In order to achieve this, make sure you don't put your puppy under undue stress during your walks. If you tense up when you're about to meet a new dog, so will he. Dogs can feel out emotions and there's no way to hide, so try to stay relaxed. Don't ever pressure them to meet or spend time with a dog if they don't seem happy to, and don't allow them to spend time with dogs which are rude or aggressive themselves. If things get heated, never scold or violently tug at your dog. While that may stop him at the moment, it won't produce any lasting educational benefits. Instead, keep calm and keep walking.

Unless you specifically have a reason for wanting your puppy to interact with another dog, it's perfectly fine to pass by calmly without greeting them. In fact, you should practice keeping your puppy's attention on you while other dogs are passing by. It's much better to offer controlled interaction with dogs that you know and trust rather than allow your puppy to insist on meeting every single dog on the street.

One of the most important things to keep in mind when it comes to preventing puppies from turning into aggressive dogs is that you can't be aggressive with them. No matter how frustrating it can be, shouting, hitting, or shaking your dog is only going to make the situation worse and has never fixed any problems. At most, your dog will fear you and he will behave, but you will have no relationship at all. You want your dog to look at you as a wise leader, not a frightening jailer.

Finally, if none of these tips seem to work, don't hesitate to contact your local canine education center and ask for help. Unwanted aggression in dogs is not something to toy with, and nothing can compare to expert help and advice. A good education center can even help you improve the situation for adult dogs which have deeply rooted problems, so a puppy should be no worry at all. Remember that all progress is made over time, in incremental steps. Don't believe any well-intended advice from people who think they have the instant cure to aggression problems.

3.5 Shy, reactive, and fearful dogs

One of the greatest difficulties for a new puppy parent can be having to care for a shy, reactive, and fearful dog. It's always a shock when you expect to have crazy adventures with your canine pal and instead you find him jumping at every shadow. And while some dogs end up having reactivity problems because of a lack of socialization or traumatic experiences, it's also completely possible that you got a puppy who is naturally shy and reactive. It's not his fault, it's just who he is.

Recognizing symptoms of a reactive puppy early is key. As you take your daily walks, take note if he seems to jump at the sight of people and dogs, if he growls at them, or if he tries to back away. Pay attention to how he reacts around dark shadows, tunnels, moving objects, wind, or any other potential trigger. Spotting a fearful dog isn't hard, he will probably make it very clear to you, but just to make sure you know what you're looking at, here are the classic signs:

- Excessive licking of the lips

- Ears flat and set back

- Tail down, between the legs. Rear end curved

- The whole spine curved

- Usually positioned sideways respective to the object of his fear

- Low growling

While it can be sad and disheartening to see that tail constantly between his legs, those ears constantly flat, and that back constantly arched, don't panic. There are many ways in which you can help a fearful, reactive puppy reach a greater level of calm and confidence. There's no reason why, through education and care, he can't end up having a perfectly normal and healthy life!

The first thing you need to do is teach your dog a very fun game called "look at it". This very simple game is going to quickly turn things around for your reactive pup. Here's how it works:

Look at it

Take a walk with your dog near an area where you know they might have a lot of triggers, such as a large park. Find yourself a comfortable spot somewhere far away from everyone else, but just far enough that you can still see them.

Settle down comfortably and wait for some people or dogs to pass by – whatever it is that triggers him. As soon as he looks at one – don't even wait one second, your timing has to be perfect – tell him "yes" and give him a treat. Feel free to substitute "yes" for "good boy" or a clicker if that's what you're using. At first, your dog won't know what to make of it, but he will be happy for the treat.

He will look back towards the frightening thing. Say "yes" and give him a reward. Every time he looks at something scary, the very next instant you have to be there to reward him. Slowly, over time, this is going to make a major shift in your dog – instead of being frightened, he is going to be cautious but happy because he knows a treat is coming. You are doing something called "counter-conditioning", or changing his negative association with an event or object into a positive one. The frightening experience becomes a game to him.

Over time, after many repetitions and many days, you will notice that your dog looks at something that scares him, and then immediately looks back towards you expecting his reward. This is a major milestone. Celebrate!

. . .

Confidence gaining for fearful dogs

Once you start working on counter-conditioning those reactions, you should also build up your puppy's confidence in parallel. A confident puppy is going to have far less of a problem walking down the street, and with enough confidence, his fear issues could disappear entirely.

The first step is to help him gain confidence by having a period of time in which nothing frightening happens. You have to break the cycle before healing can begin and there are many things you can do to help:

- avoid crowds and strange dogs

- use your body to act as a shield between your dog and frightening things

- use a crate when strangers come to visit

- use quiet and deserted streets for your walks

- don't be shy in telling people not to approach you or your dog

Try to keep your puppy calm and happy in any way you can without reinforcing his fears that the world is a big bad place.

Always let your dog set the pace. This holds true for all puppies, but especially fearful ones. Be patient and listen to them. They will make it clear when they're not ready for a certain situation or encounter – don't push them. They need to build confidence in themselves and they won't do that by constantly being in uncomfortable situations. More importantly, they need to have faith in you and know that you will care for them.

The next step in confidence building is playing games. One of the most therapeutic games for a dog is tug-of-war. Playing tug-of-war with you gives them a great workout, but also strengthens their bond with you, heightens their natural instincts and builds their self-confidence. If you play it right, you can teach your dog a great number of things by playing tug. So how do you do it?

Tug-of-war

Start off with a rag, or something soft and easy to bite. Keep in mind that the mouth of a young puppy is quite small. Get down on the floor in a room with no distractions and start gently moving the rag about left and right and playing with it yourself. When your puppy starts to be interested, move it away from him to encourage his chasing instincts. Most puppies will take to this game instantly and bite the rag, pulling on it. With some, it takes longer. Make sure there is nothing distracting or frightening them and persevere! If they seem fearful, try to tie the rag to a string and stand further away from your puppy.

When your puppy gets the rag in his mouth, keep it moving. Moving targets are interesting, still ones are not. The moment you stop moving it, he will start chewing it or let it go entirely. Move it in such a way that if he tries to chew it, he loses it! When you see that he has a good solid grip and is holding on tightly, let him win. Show him that he is brave and strong by pretending that he beat you every now and then.

This would also be a good opportunity to teach your puppy the command "drop it". It's another bonus to playing tug-of-war and a great command to have on hand when you need to get something your dog is holding in his mouth. Besides, every new chance you get to understand each other better is valuable!

To teach "drop it" start by playing tug. When your puppy has a firm grip on the toy, move your hands so that they are quite close to his mouth and there's not much toy visible. The trick is to then stop the toy completely. One good way to do this is to put your hands (with the toy) in your lap. Your puppy will give one or two tugs, trying to figure out why the toy is no longer moving. Say "drop it" and wait. Sometimes it takes seconds, sometimes minutes, but if you keep that toy completely immobile, sooner or later he will let go and look at you. That's when you should say "yes" and immediately start playing again.

The more you repeat this, the faster he will get at letting go of the toy on command. It's a very easy trick and one too few puppy parents teach.

One final thought on shy, reactive, and fearful dogs: never punish them for being afraid. You're going to make matters much worse very quickly and there's no point. Kindness and love will take you much further down the road of understanding than anger will.

3.6 Separation anxiety

Before we talk about how to prevent and deal with separation anxiety, let's take a moment to make sure that we are all on the same page when it comes to what separation anxiety actually means. There are many things which look like separation anxiety but aren't, and your dog may very well be suffering from one of these.

What separation anxiety is

Separation anxiety is when your dog is in extreme distress from the moment you leave until the moment you return. No matter what you do, he won't calm down. Leaving him a pound of steak or the most delicious bone in the world on the floor wouldn't distract him. The company of another pet wouldn't distract him. Not even being exhausted from a five-hour walk would help – he needs to be close to you and that's it. As you can see, in reality, when people think they're dealing with separation anxiety, they almost never are. So what other things look like separation anxiety and how can we fix them?

The most common answer is boredom. In 99% of cases where puppy owners think it's separation anxiety, it's really just boredom. A bored puppy, when left alone, will find something to entertain himself with. He will bark, howl, or whine the entire time. He will chew up the furniture. He will pee on your shoes. In some extreme cases, they can easily get so agitated as to chew on their own feet or tail to the point of drawing blood. It can seem absolutely gruesome… and yet it's just boredom.

So how do you test if that's the case? Easy. Leave a hunk of steak in the room with him and leave the house for ten minutes. When you come back, is the steak gone? Then it's probably not separation anxiety. A dog suffering from anxiety would never be able to settle down and eat.

If boredom is the problem, the answer is simple but usually unpleasant for new puppy parents. You need to spend more time exercising your dog. You need to give him physical exercise by way of fetch and tug, mental exercise by way of obedience training, and stimulating new things to interact with by way of walks. There's no way around it, so you might as well accept it: puppies take a lot of time. Set up a healthy routine, consider leaving him alone in a controlled environment where he can't do damage and leave him with a Kong or other puzzle toy to keep him busy. Don't forget the chew toys!

So let's say you tried the "hunk of steak" test and he didn't eat it. Does that mean that he's suffering from separation anxiety? Maybe not. There's still another option to consider. It's possible that your dog isn't suffering from separation anxiety, but from a similar issue called "isolation anxiety". Isolation anxiety is when a dog has an issue with being left alone. It's not about you personally, it's just about being deprived of all stimuli. So how can you test if what you're dealing with is isolation anxiety? Easy. Leave the house, but leave your dog with another person or dog for ten minutes. If he's still equally agitated, it's separation anxiety – he can't be separated from you. If he's fine, it's probably just about isolation.

A dog that has trouble handling isolation can be helped in several ways. The obvious solution is to make sure he's not isolated when you go away. Having another person stop by frequently to play with him would help, as would having the company of other pets. In many cases, even just having entertainment makes a difference: a window to look out of and see people passing by, a TV left on the animal channel, a radio left on soothing music. Combining this with the previous advice for boredom should do the trick. A well-exercised puppy which is tired and happy is less likely to suffer from isolation anxiety as well.

If you've eliminated all of the other options, then perhaps the only one you're left with is separation anxiety. Often, separation anxiety will have all of the symptoms of boredom and isolation anxiety, but with a few added behaviors:

- nervous pacing as you prepare to leave

- whining and trembling

- howling the entire time you're gone

- nervous licking of the lips and excessive salivation

- desperate attempts to escape confinement, often resulting in heavy property damage and injury to your dog

What causes separation anxiety?

Separation anxiety is not "bad behavior" since the dog has no control over his reaction whatsoever. In that sense, it's much more similar to human depression than anything else. And much like human depression, the causes can often be obscure and varied.

Some puppies are simply more prone to suffering from separation anxiety than others. They are born that way. They will form a strong attachment and dependence to you quickly and struggle to let go of it. There's nothing you can do to identify puppies that have this problem before it actually manifests itself.

Sometimes dogs that come from shelters have this problem. Being abandoned once can have lasting traumatic effects on a dog. Puppies that are never left alone during their first few months of life can develop this problem. Puppies that are left alone too much or too abruptly can also suffer from it. Or a puppy can experience all of these things and yet never have separation anxiety.

What can you do about separation anxiety?

Understand that there is no quick fix for this problem. There's no solution that will immediately "fix" your dog, so be wary of taking friendly advice from people who claim that. Start by putting into practice all of the other advice mentioned under "boredom" and "isolation anxiety". Depending on your individual dog, many of those things will help and, at the very least, they can't hurt. Always start working on separation anxiety problems with a well-exercised, tired dog.

1. Desensitization

At the moment, your dog is very sensitive to your leaving the house. We need to start by making him less so through a process of "desensitization". This implies replacing at least some of his fears with positive emotions. If he begins to get agitated whenever you put on your shoes, try putting on your shoes a couple of times a day without leaving the house. Put them on and then give him a delicious treat instead. Then take them off and go on with your day. Repeat that many times a day, for many days, until putting on your shoes makes him happy instead of upset. Do the same thing for any action that starts to agitate him. Try to give him an extra special treat just as you're about to walk out the door – something truly irresistible, preferably on an empty stomach. It's perfectly fine to have your dog skip a meal in preparation for receiving something delicious when you leave the house. While you should always try to keep his feeding times regular, separation anxiety is a serious problem and warrants some serious measures.

2. Countering excessive attachment

It's a great thing to have a close bond with your dog, but you're not doing him any favors by encouraging his excessively clingy behavior. Try to be relaxed around him and keep him busy when you're in the house. Get him used to not always being in the same room as you, even if you have to start with only a minute at a time. Get used to resisting his incessant requests for attention. It's cute when you're working at your desk and he puts his head on your knee, but if you cuddle him at that moment you may just be reinforcing his separation anxiety. Avoid getting emotional whenever you leave the house or return home; treat it instead like a completely relaxed situation. Don't even greet your dog before leaving or when you get home. Greeting him enthusiastically as soon as you get home may reinforce his anxieties. Take your time, settle down, and when he's calmer go in for a scratch.

3. Crate training

On top of every other good reason to crate train, it can also help with separation anxiety. A tired, well-exercised puppy that's put in his crate is much more likely to calmly chew his toys or nap when you are away. Think about what it's like for people suffering from anxiety: having the ability to pace nervously, looking out the window every two seconds to see who is coming, or running around fretting is often only going to make you feel more anxious. Certainly, pacing has never helped anyone calm down. It's better to not give your puppy the option to fall into these self-perpetuating, anxiety-inducing habits. A crate will also keep him safer, just make sure it's solidly constructed and well shut. Be sure to check whether your dog actually feels safer and calmer in the crate, as the opposite effect has been known to happen to certain dogs.

4. Other aides

Supplements and homeopathic treatments can sometimes help with the healing process if taken in combination with other helpful techniques described in this chapter. Check with your vet before you give your dog any supplements.

Medication is also an option, but it should really only be a last resort option. Even if your veterinarian is willing to prescribe it, remember that we live in a very Prozac-happy era. Don't go there unless you've tried everything else first.

Some people swear by calming pheromone diffusers. It's very hard to gather statistics on separation anxiety, so there's no guaranteed irrefutable proof that they work at all. Check out the reviews, try them for yourself, and see what the results are, if any.

Even more commonly, people recommend the Thunder-Shirt. This is a canine garment designed to help with dogs who are afraid of loud thunder and other noises, but it seems to have a calming effect that can extend to many other situations such as visits to the vet or being left home alone. This is another product that you can't be sure about until you try it on your dog. Many swear it has miraculous effects, though, so it's worth considering.

Finally, remember that separation anxiety is a tough issue to treat. It may not even be possible for you to improve the situation by yourself, and if that is the case, you shouldn't hesitate to talk to a canine behaviorist or a veterinarian and ask for their help. There's no shame in needing expert advice for a serious problem, just don't wait too long to ask for it.

3.7 Final thoughts

Having a puppy enter your life changes everything. It will

be a roller-coaster of emotions from beginning to end. You may end up suffering from every single hardship known to puppy kind, or you may sail through the experience with no problems. It's important to remember that no matter how hard it gets, neither you nor your puppy is "broken" or "bad", and no problem is so great that you can't work on it. Through persistence, patience, and help from professionals, even the most stubborn dog can become an obedient, loving pet. Don't give up on them and yourself.

Lots of puppies end up abandoned at the shelter because of many of the problems described in this book. In almost all cases, all it would have taken to turn the situation around is a little patience, love, and willingness to put in the time. There's one thing you can be sure of, though: you will be rewarded for the effort that you put in with love, companionship, and adventures.

PART II

ADULT TRAINING

4

PUPPIES AND ADULTS – WHAT'S THE DIFFERENCE?

Having a dog can be a wonderful, life-changing experience. It's important to understand, however, that there are quite a lot of differences between opening your home to a puppy, an adult dog, or an elderly dog. They take different levels of commitment and have different requirements.

There are advantages and disadvantages to both puppies and adult dogs. On the one hand, puppies are fun and exciting, and raising them yourself gives you the opportunity to educate them the way you like and make sure they fit into your household perfectly. On the other hand, they require so much more attention than you suspect!

An adult dog, on the other hand, has already gone through most of its formative years. You don't have to worry as much about things like unwanted chewing or potty training, and his energy levels will have balanced out somewhat. However, if you didn't educate him yourself, there's a good chance that there will be lots of odd or unfortunate behaviors in his repertoire which you will need to solve. It's often a lot harder to fix these issues later on than it is to simply prevent them from happening in puppyhood, and that's the main reason why most people would rather adopt a younger dog.

4.1 When does a dog become an adult?

The age at which a puppy becomes an adult differs from breed to breed and can range between one and three years old. A Labrador is considered an adult at two and a half to three years for males and at two years for females. There's often a long period in between the two in which a puppy is a teenager, and that comes with all the behavior problems and difficulties you'd expect from a human teenager as well.

While there are breed charts that show the different age at which different breeds mature, it's always possible that you have a mixed breed or unknown breed puppy and can't rely on any of those numbers. It's important, therefore, to have a rough idea of what you can expect to see when your pup becomes an adult.

From a physical point of view, your puppy has become an adult when he is fully grown, has reached his optimal height and weight, and is ready to breed. Most dogs will reach this point at around six to eight months old, and this is considered sexual maturity.

Mentally and emotionally, you can say that your dog is an adult when he becomes fully integrated into your household, his energy levels are balanced, his daily routine established, and he has a set position in the hierarchy of your family. This is also the point at which their hormonal surges even out and they start to show off their adult personality. You will usually know when he is "all grown up" because he will become less of a pest and more the companion that you always hoped he would be.

If handled properly, puppy problems such as unwanted chewing, nipping, or disobedience will also fade as your dog becomes an adult. They become better at interacting with you, other dogs, and the world around them.

4.2 Differences in training

Have you ever heard the saying "You can't teach an old dog new tricks"? Well, it is absolutely not true. Dogs of any age, even elderly ones, can and should learn new things all the time. However, there are a number of differences between training your puppy and training an adult dog.

A puppy will pretty much be open to anything. He's a sponge for education and will be quick in picking up any habits you allow him to learn, good or bad.

Depending on where he was raised and how, an adult dog may already know a lot of the essentials of being a dog. It's also possible that he has bad habits which you will have to un-train before you can retrain the good ones.

An older dog doesn't absorb information as quickly as a puppy does, but that doesn't make them less teachable. It might even be better for first time owners because an older dog is also more forgiving of mistakes during training than a puppy would be. You need to be armed with more patience, but you can also enjoy much more patience on his part. Puppies have short attention spans and need very short, frequent training sessions. An adult dog can go at a slower pace for a longer time.

Training a puppy usually focuses around socialization, the process by which you acclimate your new friend to the outside world and everything in it. An adult dog will have already, for better or worse, made up his mind about what is dangerous and what isn't, as well as whether he trusts people, dogs, children, cars, and anything else he's encountered. In the case of a well educated, well-adjusted dog, this can be a serious blessing. But if there are any negative associations in his past, you will need to re-train and re-socialize your adult dog, which is more difficult than training a puppy.

The one thing that both have in common is that you have to begin from the basics. Both puppies and adult dogs need to know the very basic commands before moving on to any fun or interesting tricks, and you can't assume that they will already know them just because they are older. Even potty training must be started from zero when you first introduce a dog into your household, no matter his age.

In short, while training a puppy is all about teaching your new friend about the world around him, training an adult dog is often about detecting and solving the problems that have come up during his formative years. Up next, we're going to talk more about the most common problems and what you can do about them. Both experiences are beautiful and challenging, and neither should deter you from inviting a new friend into your home!

5

SUPPLIES AND COSTS

One of the most important things to remember when you bring a dog into your life is that dogs are huge investments, both in terms of time and in terms of finances; and if for some reason you're not sure you can afford one or the other, it would be better to reconsider.

It's always good to plan ahead, so in this next chapter, we're going to break down what items you need to buy and replace for your dog throughout his life and why each of them is important. This list isn't exhaustive, there are for sure many other things you could buy, but these are the basics that will be enough for most owners and their dogs. Prices are approximate, based on current Amazon prices at the date of publishing, but they should be enough to give you an idea of what you can expect. It's always a good idea to wait for special offers if you can, but do try to get good quality items as much as possible.

5.1 Shelter

One of the most important things you can sort out for your

dog when he first arrives is his shelter. No, we're not talking about a doghouse outside – your dog belongs in the house with you at night, otherwise what you're really looking for is a burglar alarm. What you need is a dog crate or carrier that will be his home whenever you're on the road, when he's at the vet, when you need to keep him safe for a few hours, when he's recovering from an injury, and potentially every night.

Why is a crate important? Most of the reasons mentioned above have to do with health and safety. At the very least, your dog should be crate trained because it's by far the safest way for him to travel. During a car crash, crates for dogs are as important as seat-belts are for us, and there is no substitute that's as safe.

The other thing you might want to consider is that crate training is the single most efficient way to potty train your puppy or adult dog, as well as a healthy way of acclimating your puppy to sleeping through the night by himself.

However you decide to handle the sleep and potty training for your puppy, you will still need a crate for all the other reasons. This should be a one time purchase. If you have a puppy, buy a crate that is the correct size for his expected adult weight, and use a divider to make it smaller on the inside if you need to until he grows into it.

A basic crate can cost you anything between $50 and $150 depending on the size of your dog, but if you buy the right size and keep it clean, there's no reason why it shouldn't last you a lifetime.

In order to turn it into a comfortable sleeping place, you will also need bedding. Puppies tend to have trouble with impulse control and chewing. So if you go right out and buy comfortable dog pillows from day one, there's a good chance you will go through a lot of them and waste a lot of money before puppyhood is over. You could simply start with old towels or rags and work your way up to more comfortable bedding when you're sure that your dog won't cause it to explode. A decent quality dog pillow will cost you around $20.

5.2 Food and water

The next most important things to get for your dog are food and water bowls. Invest upfront in good quality, stainless steel bowl and you only have to make the purchase once. Besides, stainless steel is easy to clean and keep bacteria-free.

A large water bowl and a food bowl that's just the right size are your basic requirements. On top of that, you might want to consider buying an extra no-splash bowl for the car, if you intend on taking a lot of trips. These three items could cost you anything between $10 and $40.

If you want to splurge, you can always buy a foldable travel cup for your walks and a water fountain, but these items are absolutely not necessary and most dogs can do without them just fine.

Dogs can drink plain tap water with no problems, so that shouldn't significantly impact your finances, however, food is another matter entirely.

The bigger your dog, the more he will eat. Many pet owners think that they can skimp on dog food by buying cheap, supermarket brands, but the reality is that you end up paying the difference in health issues and veterinary bills later on. High quality, high protein, no filler food is absolutely crucial in order to help your dog grow up properly and stay healthy. You should find the best dry kibble you possibly can and follow the recommended dose religiously. Keep in mind that the dose recommended on the package is often exaggerated in order to make you buy more food. Look it up in various places to be sure. Depending on the size of your dog, feeding him a good quality food can cost anywhere from $250 to $700 a year. It's not much in terms of human food prices, but it's something to consider.

5.3 Walking gear

The next most important thing is your walking gear. It's inevitable that you will take your dog out for walks and hopefully for fun adventures as well. Having him wear the right equipment is crucial for his safety and your comfort.

Nowadays, most people are steering away from collars and towards harnesses – and rightfully so. A harness offers more comfort and security without any risk while a collar is a tool that can be easily misused by a beginner owner with an energetic dog. Feel free to buy a collar for beauty or in order to attach a tag to it, but don't expect to attach the leash to it much if ever.

Instead, you will need to find a harness. They come in different types and sizes and if your dog is a puppy, you will need to buy more than one as he outgrows them. They are adjustable, but you can still expect to change two or three before he's done growing, and then use up about one every couple of years for the rest of his life depending on the quality.

You can get a decent harness that won't last longer than a year from any pet store for $15 to $30, but it's really better to invest in a high-quality sports harness from a reputable brand. These can go for $75 to $150, but there's a good chance you can get three to five years of heavy use out of them.

Next up, you're going to need a leash. A sturdy leash made out of paracord can last you for a very long time and costs as little as $5, so consider that option wisely before investing in fancy bejeweled leashes. You will need a standard length, a 5 feet (1.5 meter) leash for city walks, but it would also be very nice to have an extra-long, 30 foot (10 meter) sports leash for when you're at the beach or in the woods. This will cost you about $20.

5.4 Chews and toys

Depending on how energetic your dog is, it's possible that you will blow through chewy things and toys at an alarming rate. No matter the breed, there are a few basic items you should always have in your arsenal. It bears mentioning that all toys should be dog safe. Be especially wary of tennis balls because real tennis balls are coated in an abrasive material that will wear your dog's teeth down very quickly. Fake tennis balls bought from the pet store are an entirely different material.

When it comes to toys, keep a couple of appropriately-sized balls, a frisbee, a few tug ropes, and some squeaky toys. These toys are strictly for playing with you and your dog should not be left alone to chew on them.

Chewing needs should be satisfied by a good supply of things like rawhide bones, antlers, cured sinew, dried bovine ears, and other natural chewy dog treats. Depending on how much energy your dog has, you could be consuming a lot of these. Between toys and chews, expect to spend another $200 to 300 per year on your dog.

5.5 Grooming

Grooming is something you could potentially consider outsourcing, but be prepared to spend a good deal of money on it if you do, especially in the case of a high maintenance dog. Alternatively, you can take care of all the grooming needs your dog has right at home by buying a few sturdy tools and learning how to use them.

You will need a durable brush that is the right type for your dog's coat. All coats are different and not all brushes work on all coats. If it seems like yours isn't picking up any hair at all, it's possible that you got the wrong type.

You should also invest in a stainless steel, high quality pair of dog nail clippers. Human clippers will absolutely not suffice. You will also need a toothbrush or finger brush for your dog.

Finally, you will have to keep a steady supply of toiletries such as shampoo or wet wipes. Don't worry though, you're supposed to use very small quantities of shampoo and the bottles don't cost very much, so you get a lot of bang for your buck.

Between all these basic grooming supplies, considering the occasional need to replace a brush, you might expect to spend under $80 a year on this category. That's certainly nowhere near as much as going to a groomer, however, it will take a lot more time and effort. You have to learn how to do it properly or risk upsetting or frightening your dog.

5.6 Puppy-specific needs

If you're bringing a puppy into your home, there may be a

few extra things you might need at some point. None of these are absolute essentials, but more often than not they can help with the difficult phase in which your dog seems to want to either chew on or pee on everything he sees.

A bottle of bitter apple spray, together with good training, can help you keep your pup away from things he really shouldn't be chewing like the carpet, the power cords, or your shoes. You will also need a bottle or two of enzymatic cleaner.

An enzymatic cleaner is the only cleaner that properly removes all the urine molecules your dog tries to leave behind. Dogs tend to pee where they can smell that they've already done so in the past, so eliminating that smell completely is crucial to your potty training efforts. You should immediately clean all accidents with an enzymatic cleaner to make sure your pup isn't tempted to go again in the same place.

Speaking of potty training, you might want to have a few puppy pee pads on hand. Even if you potty train outdoors – which is the best way to do it – you never know when you will have an ill or injured puppy who will need a little extra help or some extra padding in his crate.

All of these items will cost you around $50 total.

5.7 Miscellaneous items

A few other small items will for sure make their way into your tool kit. You will need poop bags that come in small rolls and cost very little. You can get a three-pack for $2 and depending on how much you walk, that could potentially last you for a few months.

You will also need a soft, textile muzzle for about $15. You may not have any intention to ever muzzle your dog, but it is an essential thing to have in case of an emergency, if your vet or groomer ever need to perform any tricky procedures, or if your state requires that you carry a muzzle with you at all times.

Having a dedicated towel for your dog is a must, and any standard towel will do and shouldn't set you back more than $5. Also, depending on how active you intend to be, there's always the chance that you might need a warm winter jacket for him. Depending on the size of your dog and the quality of the jacket, this can cost anywhere from $20 to $150. Of course, cheaper options are available and with a little skill, you can easily make a warm sweater for your dog out of one of your old sweaters.

If you are at all crafty, other things such as bedding and tug toys can also be improvised. Just be sure that whatever you use, it's clean, safe for his mouth, and you don't leave him with it unsupervised.

5.8 Veterinary costs

Medical costs can be the most expensive part of pet ownership, no matter the pet in question. Naturally, it's impossible to predict what kind of medical emergencies your dog might have – anything from broken limbs to food poisoning can be very expensive, not to mention more serious life-threatening conditions. However, there are some standard costs you can anticipate even if your dog will always be in perfect health.

An average vet checkup can run between $50 and $200, and if you need any vitamins, you can expect to pay around $50 a year. You will need flea and tick prevention, which runs in the area of $20 per month. Yearly vaccines are essential and, including the rabies vaccine, can reach up to $200 a year.

You will also have a few one-time costs. You need to microchip your dog and, depending on where you live, that can either be free or cost up to $100. You might also be thinking of spaying or neutering your pet, which usually costs around $100 to $300 depending on the size of the dog and the quantity of anesthetic required.

If you don't spay or neuter your pet, you're not off the hook. There's a very good chance you will eventually have to deal with the costs related to breeding and having puppies. That cost can vary wildly depending on whether or not you keep them yourself, whether you have the male or female, whether the pregnancy and delivery go smoothly, how many puppies there are, and a whole host of other factors. We talk more about this topic in our chapter about breeding!

You can learn most of this information from your vet on your first visit. The moment you get a new dog, be it an adult or a puppy, the first thing you have to do is set up a vet visit. The vet will check his health status, de-worm him, give him his first shots, and explain to you what the overall schedule for vaccinations is. Don't be afraid to ask for details about prices and remember to get their emergency number or the number of a local 24-hour emergency service for animals.

6

AGING AILMENTS OF DOGS

One of the things that you have to be prepared for when bringing a dog into your life is the fact that sooner or later you will have an elderly dog. Elderly dogs can come with many problems, both physical and behavioral, and you have to be prepared to give them extra care, attention, and patience. There's no way around it, and you have to treat your elderly dog the way you expect to be treated when you are old.

Here are some of the most common ailments that elderly dogs suffer from. This is by no means an exhaustive list, but it should give you a rough idea of what you can expect so that you can better prepare.

6.1 Arthritis

Like people, dogs too can develop arthritis in their old age. Arthritis is a disease of the joints characterized by pain and swelling. There is a degenerative variety called Osteoarthritis which is common in elderly canines. Most commonly, they will suffer from osteoarthritis in the wrists, elbows, knees, and hips.

You can ease their pain and delay the progress of osteoarthritis through diet, exercise, and pain control medication. Stem cell research has come a long way toward helping in these situations, but stem cell treatment can be very expensive and has absolutely no guarantee of success at the moment.

6.2 Kidney problems

The kidneys are often sensitive and easily damaged organs. Kidney failure, kidney stones, and chronic kidney disease can be a serious problem for old dogs. When the kidneys start to malfunction, toxins build up in the body. While it's possible to identify these issues, there is very little that can be done for them aside from slowing the progression of the disease and reducing pain.

6.3 Cancer

Just like humans, senior dogs have a chance of developing cancer. There are various kinds of cancer with many different symptoms. Between them all, cancer is actually the main cause of death for elderly dogs. Cancer can be detected during routine screenings and treatment is possible. Much like in the case of people however, treatment has a better chance of being effective if the cancer is discovered early, and it can be quite costly and difficult to go through.

6.4 Dementia

It sounds unbelievable, but elderly dogs can and do develop dementia. Much like Alzheimer's disease for us, canine dementia often starts slowly and becomes more serious over time. Sometimes it only presents as mild memory loss or disorientation, which can easily pass unnoticed. Often, it comes with serious personality changes and that could potentially be dangerous. There is no cure for canine dementia, but there are medications that can help.

6.5 Eyes and ears

Most elderly dogs will struggle with failing eyesight and hearing at some point. The nerves in the eyes and ears degenerate, or cataract sets in, and our beloved pets lose the use of one or even both these senses. Unfortunately, there isn't much that medicine can do in the case of eyesight problems or hearing problems caused by old age.

The good news is that dogs are highly adaptable and as long as we recognize what the issue is and work with them to help them, they can live a perfectly comfortable life. The symptoms are often confused with dementia because dogs that are hearing or vision impaired can often appear disoriented, grumpy, and easily startled. The first thing you need to do is understand the reasons for this change in behavior and be patient and tolerant.

Keep your dog on a leash at all times when outside and find other comforting ways to reassure him and communicate with him if you can't use your voice. Hand gestures and touches can be used just as efficiently as vocal commands.

Keep the environment stable and try not to move furniture around, or leave things in their favorite paths, as it's very likely that this will confuse and upset them. If they can learn about their environment, they can navigate it with much less trouble.

Finally, be sure that everyone in the household understands how to behave, including children and other pets. Running up behind a deaf or blind dog and startling him is under no circumstances acceptable, nor is touching him suddenly when he doesn't know you're there.

6.6 Diabetes

This disease primarily affects aging female dogs. The disease is hereditary, so if your pup has a pedigree you should have a pretty good idea of your chances. This is an illness where the body no longer produces enough insulin to regulate the transformation of glucose into energy. Symptoms include drinking more water and urinating more frequently, being irritable, and losing weight. There's no cure for it, but you can help keep it under control with a proper diet and exercise.

6.7 Heart problems

One of the common problems elderly dogs have to face is degenerative canine heart disease. About 50% of elderly dogs will have some sort of heart problems and most of those will be small dog breeds.

In younger dogs, there are surgeries and treatments that can slow or stop the progress of heart disease, but in elderly dogs, it's often advised to let it run its course.

6.8 Oral issues

Dogs interact with the world mainly by using their mouths the way we do our hands. Many of them, especially high-energy breeds, will have their teeth almost constantly working on something. It's no surprise then that after years of hard use, their teeth and gums can develop problems and begin to suffer. Keeping good oral hygiene early on can help with this. The other problem is that gum disease in an elderly dog can easily send bacteria rushing through the bloodstream and affect other weak organs such as the heart.

6.9 Obesity

We often indulge our elderly pets more than the younger ones. This isn't, however, a great idea. As dogs get older, they become less active and their nutritional requirements actually decrease instead of increasing. The quantity of food and treats should, therefore, decrease too. Obesity comes with a whole slew of unpleasant side-effects that we don't want for our dogs, like heart problems and joint issues and many others. Compared to all of these health risks, the effort of measuring proper portions and sticking to them isn't so large after all.

6.10 Other various problems

While the ones mentioned above will give you a rough idea of what you can expect, there are any number of other issues that you should be prepared for. Dogs can suffer from all kinds of growths and tumors, both benign and malign. Incontinence is also a major issue in old age which a lot of owners struggle with. Each dog is different however, so if any of these health conditions worry you, see your veterinarian and ask for details.

7

VACCINATIONS

Vaccinations seem to be a hot topic at the moment in both the human and the animal world. While the debate is still ongoing for humans, in the case of dogs the situation is much simpler: You have to vaccinate. While you can't really be forced to, there are many situations in which you will simply not be welcome without the proper documents and vaccinations, including travel abroad, competitions, shows, puppy kennels, boarding, training, etc.

While it can sometimes seem like a lot, the truth is that we vaccinate now for diseases that rippled through the canine population and killed thousands of great dogs every year before these vaccines were available. If you ever have any doubts as to whether they are important, research any one of the diseases like Leptospirosis or Bordetella. The effects of them are chilling.

It's also very likely that anyone over the age of 60 who owned dogs as a child can easily tell you stories about beloved family pets who died out of the blue, or had to be put down because of rabies contracted from a squirrel.

There is no reason why you wouldn't protect your dog from these dangers, and if vaccinations aren't something you can afford, then you can't afford a dog.

Here's a rough idea of when you can expect to vaccinate and what against:

7.1 Dog vaccination schedule

Age:

6-8 weeks – Distemper, Measles, Parainfluenza, Bordatella

10-12 weeks – Distemper, Hepatitis, Parainfluenza, Parvovirus, (these come packaged under a single vaccine called DHPP), Leptospirosis, Lyme disease, Bordatella, Coronavirus

12 to 24 weeks – Rabies (This is required by law in most places in the world)

14 to 16 weeks – DHPP booster, Lyme disease, Coronavirus, Leptospirosis

1 year – DHPP booster, Rabies, Leptospirosis, Lyme disease, Coronavirus, Bordatella

Every 1 or 2 years – DHPP booster, Coronavirus, Bordatella, Leptospirosis

Every 1 or 3 years – Rabies (This is required by law in most places in the world)

Depending on your vet, which specific brands of vaccine they use, and where in the world you are, your mileage may vary. Some companies produce vaccines that need to be renewed annually, others package the same vaccine in a way that allows it to be taken only once every three years. Some areas are more prone to some diseases and insist on those vaccinations, but may be willing to monitor immunity and vaccinate only in case of necessity for others.

The best way to know for sure is to ask your vet about his standard vaccination schedule, then do a little research regarding the diseases named and the ones prevalent in your region. You will see that usually unless the vet is a complete hack, his suggestions make sense and should be followed.

A lot of people are worried about the traumatizing effects that vaccinations can have on a dog. They are concerned that the pain of vaccination will give the dog a negative reaction to ever going to the vet and it's true – many dogs try to bolt the moment they realize where they are going.

However, we need to be clear on one thing. It is mishandling by the owner and veterinarian which causes the problem, not the vaccination itself. The shot takes moments to administer, it's given in areas which are not very sensitive at all – usually between the shoulder blades – and a happy, healthy dog can easily go through vaccinations without any sort of negative reaction or fear at all.

This implies that both the owner and the vet are calm, handle the matter quickly and efficiently with minimal stress to the animal, use positive reinforcement and copious rewards throughout the visit, and maintain an atmosphere of relaxed cheerfulness. Dogs can pick up on our feelings very easily and it's usually the reason why they get stressed – we are telling them to be worried.

An agitated, fearful owner that uses force rather than

rewards to get the dog through the veterinary visit is sure to cause a dog that hates these visits and will only struggle more with them each time. This isn't because the vaccines are unbearably painful – on the contrary, they're almost painless. It's because we mishandled the situation.

7.2 How to have a calm dog from the very first vet visit

Whether you have a puppy or an adult dog, whether they're already terrified of the vet or don't even know the concept yet, these are the steps you need to follow if you want things to go smoothly and be fear and pain-free for both you and your beloved pet.

1. Don't make a huge fuss. It's like going to get a massage. It's good for your health, a relaxing experience, and sure, some of the techniques might be a bit rough, but that's part of the fun. Taking care of your dog's health should be no more stress-inducing than a massage.

2. Pack treats and toys. If your vet doesn't already reward dogs for good behavior, you absolutely should. Grab his favorite toy and some high-value treats. This is not the time for organic tofu kibble – bring out the chicken livers and venison chunks.

3. Make sure he's comfortable and his harness is set up properly, you may need to hold him still later on.

4. Play games in the waiting room. Play tug, practice tricks, or invent a whole new game. This is a great time to try out something extremely fun and easy like "Which hand is the treat in?" where your dog always wins.

5. Keep light and cheerful tones when you're in the office. Your voice should be normal and relaxed.

6. Don't dawdle. Don't put your dog up on the table and then decide to ask the vet questions about the history of tick repellents. Get things done as quickly as you can.

7. Talk to your dog the entire time he's up on the table. Reward him for sitting still and being good. If he panics, let him get off and try again later using baby steps and a lot of rewards.

8. Do something incredibly fun right after the visit is over. Play a game of fetch or go hiking for a little bit, let the most important memory of the day be of having fun in the sun rather than just getting shots.

9. Don't let up with the rewards over the next visits. It's better to use up all his calories for the day – and then skip the next meal – to keep him happy at the vet than to feed him regular meals and let visits be fear and anxiety-ridden.

7.3 Fleas and other dog parasites

There is a good chance that at some point in his life your dog will be infested with fleas or ticks. It's almost inevitable, there are so many ways in which these parasites can move from host to host. Sometimes ticks can be found on long blades of grass, just waiting for a victim to pass by. Rural areas are especially at risk of ticks, whereas fleas are much more likely to be transmitted from dog to dog in crowded city settings.

It's important to eliminate parasites quickly because an adult flea could potentially lay hundreds of eggs in a matter of days. These eggs can fall off into carpets, bedding, and floorboards, and wait for the right time to emerge. Definitely not the kind of house guest you want to have!

If your dog has fleas, you may notice them itching, scratching, chewing their paws and tail, or rubbing their bodies against the walls or furniture. They may develop red irritated patches of skin and suffer hair loss.

However, not all dogs react in this way. Some show no signs at all, and ticks usually don't produce any of these symptoms. It's important to spend regular time with your dog during cuddles checking him for parasites, especially after a romp in the wilderness or through town. There are usually hot spots where fleas tend to gather, such as under the chin, behind the ears, between the shoulders, and at the root of the tail.

If your dog has fleas, there are various commercially available products that will treat your pet as well as your carpets and home. Ask your vet for a recommendation on what best fits your situation. In the case of ticks, you should learn how to safely remove a tick from your dog with either a special tick removing tool or, better yet, a simple pair of tweezers.

Of course, prevention is better than cure in these cases. The real issue with parasites beyond discomfort is that they can be carriers of all kinds of diseases. Once the tick or flea is on your pet, he has already been exposed to that risk and removing the parasite does not nullify the effects. That's why vaccinating against tick and flea-borne diseases is crucial.

The other step you should take is to use preventative measures in order to stop this from happening at all. Fleas and ticks are external parasites, so you can prevent them from causing problems to your dog with safe products that are easy to administer by yourself. This may also include having to treat your home, carpets, bedding, curtains, etc.

Your vet will know exactly what the chances of fleas or ticks in your area are and whether you need to take preventative action. In many cases, you will only need to do so certain months a year and not others.

8

BEFORE YOU BREED

Thinking about breeding your dog? There are many joys that come with that experience, but also many things to keep in mind before you start. Let's start by looking at some of the reasons why you may or may not want to breed your dog.

1. Are you trying to breed for financial gain?

Then don't breed your dog. It's incredibly hard to make any profit at all and that usually only happens for people who do this for a living, breeding multiple dogs and having multiple litters as well as a well-established network of clients.

Even charging full price for each pup, you still need to have two perfectly healthy dogs with all the medical and legal requirements met, invest time and money in the pregnancy and whelping, and take care of the pups for the first two months. Factor in food, vaccines, microchips, surprise vet bills if the puppies have any special needs, potential complications for each pregnancy, and really you should consider yourself lucky to break even. Money should absolutely never be the main reason for breeding your dog.

2. Do you want to have the joyous experience of new life in your family?

Then don't breed your dog. The reality is that pregnancy can be a very cruel and complicated thing, and exposing your kids to stillborn or dying pups may not be exactly what you had in mind. Plus, the stress of the whelping is only going to put pressure on your family and won't feel miraculous at all.

You can have the same experience without any of the pain by going to a local kennel and volunteering to help out. Your kids can spend time there and maybe witness puppies being born in that way, or even foster newborn puppies who need socializing before being adopted into forever homes. There are many other ways of having that experience without putting more unwanted puppies in the world – honestly, there are more than enough to go around.

3. I heard that every female dog has to have at least one litter

Then don't breed your dog. Hearsay and misinformation is no excuse to take on such a complex and difficult enterprise. That statement simply isn't true, having a litter does nothing for a female in the long term other than expose her to the risk of mammary cancer. Both genders can very safely be spayed or neutered without ever having had a litter and it won't have any harmful effects on them at all.

This sort of old tale is proof in itself that just because your dog is registered and you want puppies doesn't mean you are prepared or have the knowledge to actually pull it off. You would be much better off leaving it to the professionals. If you want another dog like yours, go to the breeder you got yours from and look at pups from the same line, instead.

4. I believe breeding this dog is going to improve the breeding

Then, by all means, breed your dog. This is the one and only reason why you ever should. The world is full of unwanted dogs, there is no excuse to create more just for our own personal vanity. Dogs that we breed should always be genetically sound, mentally sound, and showing off the breed characteristics to the absolute best of their ability. They must prove themselves to external evaluation as well, so that means winning titles in competitions. They can be superior examples of their breed in beauty, obedience, agility, or any number of other categories – but they must be superior specimens in some way.

These dogs must be observed into maturity for personality issues and closely monitored for hereditary problems. Failure to do so and focusing only on beauty or skill is the main reason why many breeds have such serious genetic problems now – for example, the hip dysplasia of the German Shepherd.

8.1 Health before breeding

If you have decided to breed, you must first make sure that both the male and the female are in excellent health. They must be up to date on vaccinations and have all their documents in order. You need to be sure that they are both free from hereditary issues, as well as any transmittable diseases such as Brucellosis.

Their mental health must be up to snuff every bit as much as their physical one. You must never breed any animal that has temperament issues, is in any way aggressive, is untrustworthy around other animals or children, or has any sort of behavior problem at all. Breeding dogs should be happy, confident, relaxed, and very obedient animals.

There are tests that can help you determine if the mental health of the animal is on par with breed expectations. Many breeds have their own personalized temperament tests and there is a general Canine Good Citizen test that is open to all dogs of any breed, including mixed breeds.

You must also spend some time researching the pedigree of your dog at this point. Make sure that you only breed them with suitable mates in order to avoid unwanted genetic mutations.

Only breed mature dogs who have had all their shots and try to keep the frequency of breeding low. There's no need to put unnecessary stress on the mother.

8.2 Pregnant or nursing dogs

So you have yourself a pregnant dog? Make sure you care for her properly. She should be registered with a vet that you can call at any time in case of an emergency. He should check her and make sure she has all her shots and vitamins and everything is going smoothly at least once during the pregnancy, and more often if there is anything at all abnormal.

She will need to eat more and better quality food during the last months of pregnancy and while nursing. Nursing dogs can eat three times as much food as they normally would. Luckily, puppy food is usually formulated in such a way as to work both for puppies and for the mothers.

You need to prepare a whelping box for your soon to be mother. This should be a space that isn't much larger than she is, in a warm sheltered area, and lined with several layers of plastic tarp. Whelping tends to get very messy and it helps if you can just peel off a layer of plastic and have a decently clean surface again for a while.

As soon as she gives birth, you need to make sure she and the puppies stay clean. That's not an easy feat, so you might want to invest in some highly absorbent material to line the box with. Synthetic materials work fine, as do pine shavings. You will need to do a lot of cleaning no matter what you use.

Newborn puppies need a lot of warmth. If you see them huddled together and crying, it's likely that they are too cold. Transition to a normal temperature gradually, by decreasing their environmental temperature by only one or two degrees a day.

8.3 Puppy schedules

By four weeks the puppies are ready to leave the whelping area and will need a safe, confined pen in which to play and interact. At this age, they are tornadoes of teeth and claws, so you better have someplace for them that is completely safe and utterly indestructible.

By five weeks, you can start introducing normal food. Boil water and mix it with their puppy kibble, then let it sit for a while to get all soft and mushy. Don't expect them to eat hard kibble. This is also very useful in order to keep them hydrated. Make sure that your puppy food is top quality.

At six weeks, the vet should visit your puppies and give them their first vaccines, as well as deworm them and check for any already detectable issues such as heart murmurs.

You should also be prepared for adoption at this point, making sure that all the paperwork is in order, and all the pups are in perfect health for when they reach the age of eight weeks, and you can start placing them.

Most people don't realize what an enormous commitment a single dog is, let alone a litter of puppies. Make this decision very wisely and consider it more as an exhausting hobby than as anything you can do for fun and profit.

9

COMMON ADULT DOG BEHAVIOR PROBLEMS

All puppies are more or less the same – they chew, nip, bark, and play to more or less the same extent. They all need potty training, they all need to be supervised as much as possible. Adult dogs, on the other hand, often come with their own individual problems and needs. Depending on where your adult dog grew up and what he learned, he may completely avoid certain issues and struggle seriously with others.

There are a few important reasons why your adult dog may be experiencing behavioral problems.

9.1 Negative associations from the past

It's possible that your dog suffered some form of trauma growing up. It doesn't always seem like a big deal, but often something as simple as getting a scare from a sudden noise or having someone step on his tail at the wrong time can, if left untreated, become an issue that you have to deal with later on in life. Negative associations can cause your dog to be reactive, fearful, to refuse to participate in activities, to seem distracted or aloof, or to be downright angry at inexplicable things.

9.2 Accidentally reinforced behavior

It often happens that we think we are rewarding our puppy for one thing and they think they're being rewarded for something entirely different. We either communicate badly or our timing is off and suddenly we have unwanted behavioral problems. A classic example is that of a dog who barks for attention. Eventually, after enough barking, we give in and go check on him "just to tell him to shut up". This is, in fact, a reward for your dog and what you're doing is inadvertently reinforcing the barking which you're trying to discourage. Another example is a puppy who performs the command "sit", but then stands up again in order to get his treat. You think you are rewarding him for sitting in the first place, but he thinks he is being rewarded for being restless and standing up again.

9.3 Normal aging

As your dog ages, he will go through multiple changes in personality. Hormones go crazy and then even out, his energy levels rise and fall, and he needs to test the boundaries of your leadership. This is a normal part of growing up and of becoming an adult.

Most of the dogs returned to shelters are sent back during this "teenager" phase where they are testing the limits of your patience. Sweet puppies who used to come when you called them suddenly no longer respond to any commands, tricks that they once knew are completely forgotten, and they just seem to not like you as much as they did before.

Like with any teenager, a rebellious stage is a natural part of the process and should be treated with love and patience.

9.4 Your rewards aren't up to snuff

It seems simple, but many owners get this wrong. Even if your puppy used to be happy to work for kibble or bits of chicken, that may not always be the case. Puppies are notoriously hungry and adult dogs quickly become more discerning in their tastes. You can't expect your dog to perform if you're not rewarding him properly, so experiment until you find a treat or prize that he really is willing to jump through hoops for.

9.5 You got mad and lost your patience

It's perfectly normal. Training sessions, especially with puppies, can be frustrating and exhausting. Often, things don't go the way you plan for absolutely no reason. Your pup seems stubborn and it feels like he's not making any progress. It's perfectly normal for both of you to sometimes get frustrated. However, in these situations, the only right answer is to stop what you're doing, take five, play with a ball or tug toy, throw some treats around, and generally raise the good mood of both yourself and your canine friend. If you get upset and shout or show your frustration in any way, your canine companion will feel it and may just decide that training sessions with you aren't all that fun and he'd rather not listen. And can you blame him?

9.6 You spoil him

Let's face it, they're adorable and manipulative. They pick up on our "oohs" and "ahhs" and know exactly which faces to pull when they want extra scraps from the table. The problem is that the more you give in to their manipulation, the more you're spoiling them and entitling them to behave however they want. You need to set out clear goals before you start working with a dog – no eating scraps from the table, no getting up on the couch, only gets the reward when he sits nicely for a few seconds – and then stick to those goals no matter what. Giving in to pleading and puppy eyes can seem sweet to you now, but when your adult dog knows no other way of communication except for demanding things from you all the time, it's not pleasant.

9.7 Mixed signals

This is a major problem in most households. Maybe you're doing everything right and raising your puppy the way you should, reinforcing positive behavior, sticking to the rules, and training daily. But what happens if the other members of your household aren't doing the same? If your rule is that the puppy has to sit nicely before being allowed up on the couch, but your kids let him up and down as he pleases, then that's not a real rule; it's a mixed signal. Mixed signals are opportunities for confusion and mistakes later on in life when your dog doesn't understand exactly which rule to obey. Mixed signals don't belong in a happy home with a happy dog. Be sure that everyone is on the same page and that you're firm about the rules you set.

MOST COMMON ADULT DOG CONCERNS AND HOW TO FIX THEM

10.1 Help! My dog isn't listening to me anymore!

If a previously well-behaved pup suddenly stops obeying your commands, there's a chance something is seriously wrong. The very first thing you should do is get him to a vet and ask for a general checkup. Make sure that his eyes and ears are in great shape and that his paws, tail, and teeth are all fine. Any sort of pain at all would make a dog distracted and uncooperative, let alone something serious like a broken toe or tooth.

Once you've ruled out all medical concerns, ask yourself if it's possible that your pup is still growing or towards the end of his adolescence phase. That's a normal time when you would expect to have him stop responding to your commands.

If your dog is fully grown, then is it possible that she is in heat? In the case of male dogs, being in the vicinity of a female in heat can completely throw off their behavior. For this reason, in shows and competitions, females in heat are required to perform last in order to minimize the disturbance to the other dogs.

If you've eliminated all other possible problems, then it might be that somewhere along the line your dog got mixed up and misunderstood either his role in the family or what your commands mean. There are two important steps you need to take in this case.

1. Reset all the rules and boundaries

Over time, as your dog grows older and becomes a member of the family, you naturally tend to relax the rules and be more permissive. Maybe he can come and go on the couch as he pleases, maybe he sneaks into the kitchen at mealtime and puts his head on your lap. There are no set rules for what you are or aren't allowed to teach your dog, as long as he is happy, healthy, and cared for. What works for some families may not work for others. But if you are beginning to have problems with your dog and discover that he is disobedient for no good reason, then it's time to reset all the rules back to ground zero and start over.

Just like when he was a puppy, make it a rule that there are places where he's not allowed to go or things for which he must ask nicely. Ask him to sit before he receives his meals, or shake before being allowed on the couch. Get him to wait patiently by the door while you prepare for walks. Be firm with the rules just like you would be with a young puppy. This helps re-establish hierarchy and remind your dog that you are, in fact, in charge of the resources and he does not need to make the decisions in your household.

2. Take the commands back to ground zero, too.

Figure out which of the commands your dog should know are most important to you. Does it bother you that he doesn't respond to "sit", "stay", or "come"? Does it bother you that he doesn't heel or look at you when you call his name?

Pick two or three of the most important commands and train them all over again, as if your dog had never heard of them before. Get high-value treats that you're certain he will love and go over the basic steps of "sit" or "stay" pretending like it's his first time. Chances are that by repeating basic training sessions a few times, by the end of the day you will have a dog that responds passably to those commands. If you need to repeat the process again two or three days later, do so. Don't consider your efforts wasted – every training session you do during this stage only serves to reinforce good behavior and strengthen the relationship between you and your dog.

10.2 My dog is aggressive with new family members!

This happens a lot. A wonderful, obedient, well-behaved dog has only one major problem: he refuses to accept any new members, be they human or animal, into the family. He keeps his distance, hides toys, growls, barks, becomes dominant and aggressive. He starts to snap if anyone passes near his food bowl or can't be trusted alone with the new pets.

Why does this happen? Often, your dog feels like your home is his den and the members of your family are his pack. Dogs have natural instincts set in place over thousands of years to protect the den and the pack, and it isn't easy to override these instincts. A new member of the family, while obviously important to you, can seem like just another intruder or danger to your dog.

So why don't all dogs respond negatively to new family members? While it's natural that all dogs will be a little suspicious of anyone new at first, it isn't a given that they will be aggressive. In fact, most dogs won't be. That's because most dogs will trust you to be the leader of the household and, when you introduce family members, they will simply accept your decision and fall in line. However, highly assertive, dominant, or stubborn dogs may have a much harder time accepting your judgment. If they feel that they are in charge of keeping the family safe, they will react negatively to any potential intruders and completely disregard your opinions on the matter.

One of the main things you can do to prevent this kind of problem from happening at all is to make sure your dog never feels like he is in an unstable home where he needs to be the primary decision-maker and protector. This means that all family members should be capable of setting themselves up as positive leaders and trustworthy figures. Much like any leader, family members must treat the dog the way a parent would treat a child or a teacher would treat a student – with an infinite amount of patience and understanding, but also with firm rules and boundaries. Having rules, just like having a schedule, is a healthy habit for a dog!

Being a leader doesn't mean asserting yourself in any negative way. Old dominance myths have been debunked and we now know that dogs coexisting with humans are not at all like wolves in the wild and do not, in fact, operate under the same principles. Being a leader means giving a positive example and rewarding good behavior so as to encourage more of that behavior in the future. It also means being able to be in control of your dog and being present to offer supervision as much as necessary. A dog that spends too much time alone will automatically assume that he doesn't have a leader and fill that position himself.

How can we treat aggression towards family members once it happens?

The first step is to assess exactly how serious the situation is. It's always terrifying to be face to face with an angry dog, more so if he injures you. But is it always automatic that if a dog bites, you should isolate him or send him away? Absolutely not. There are a million reasons why a dog might resort to aggression and most of them are well within your power to improve upon.

Here are some steps you can take:

1. Start by establishing which situations cause your dog stress and provoke negative reactions. Is it when someone walks into the house? Is it triggered by someone in particular or by any stranger? Is it when they get too close to the food bowl?

2. Decide what you do want him to do, instead of reacting aggressively. You can't simply tell a dog not to do something, they don't have the option to watch a movie or read a book instead. You have to have a plan in place of what you want him to do, even if it's something as simple as sitting or going to his pillow. Train and reinforce this behavior heavily at first, without introducing the problematic stimulus.

3. Introduce the stimulus. Once you've trained your dog to, for example, go to his sleeping spot on command and happily, it's time to introduce the stimulus. Whether it's the doorbell ringing, someone walking in the room, or someone walking past his food bowl, the method is the

same. Start slowly. Introduce the stimulus either from very far away or much more slowly than usual, and get your dog to perform the desired action. Reward him heavily and only increase the intensity of the stimulus very, very slowly. It will take you a few days of constant, consistent practice to get him to a level where he doesn't react even with a spontaneous event, but it's well worth the effort.

While you are training, it's always a good idea to use harnesses and soft halters to help keep everyone involved safe. Only graduate to more advanced exercises when you're absolutely sure that nobody is in any danger of injury. And if you feel like you're in over your head at any time, this is a perfectly reasonable excuse to call a specialist and ask for help! Every dog is different and while general advice might work well for mild cases or if you are instinctively a great trainer, difficult cases may require special training and consultations. There's nothing wrong with asking for help!

10.3 My dog refuses to be touched, bathed, or groomed

It's common to hear dog owners complain that they can't perform basic grooming on their dog because he refuses to be touched, to sit still, to touch water, or any number of other reasons. This can be a very serious problem because if your dog won't allow you to touch his paws for long enough to wash them, it's very unlikely you'll ever be able to perform any emergency medical treatment on him either, and that could potentially be life-threatening.

Furthermore, this suggests a more serious problem at a relationship level between you and your dog. Ideally, unless he is in any pain, your dog should trust you and be patient with you when you need to touch him. You shouldn't abuse this right, but you should also never be in a situation where you are afraid to handle your own dog.

Why are dogs skittish about being touched? There could be any number of reasons. Certainly, it's a good idea to stop by the vet and make sure his health is in order if you notice him suddenly protect certain areas. But if he's not in pain, then it's very likely that this problem comes from some form of negative association that he developed in the past. He was startled by the water, his toenail was clipped badly and it hurt him, shampoo got in his eyes – it doesn't take much to make him decide that grooming is no fun and he'd rather not have it. So what can we do in these situations?

Refusing to be bathed

If you start early enough, it's possible to make bath time a fun and pleasant experience for your pup. But even if that's not realistic in your case, you can at the very least make it a tolerable experience for both of you.

Use extremely powerful treats to lure your dog into the bath. Don't chase after him and grab him, don't drag him there by force. If he has serious issues even getting near it, then use the treats to make him come close, reward him, and let him go. Nobody says he has to make it all the way in on day one. When he's comfortable going halfway there, go a little closer. When he's comfortable being right next to it, get him inside and reward him heavily. Let him go through the motions of getting in several times before ever actually giving him a bath, and make sure to reward him like it's the most important thing he's ever done in his life. Keep a treat jar in the bathroom just for the occasion and finish all sessions with either a chew toy or a food puzzle toy which will help your dog relax and unwind as well as give him something to look forward to.

Once your dog is happy to be in the tub and you've been rewarding calm behavior for a while, you can start the process of actually bathing him. Use warm water and try not to startle him with high-pressure jets. If your dog is particularly skittish, don't even use the jet at all, instead dampen a washcloth in warm water and gently clean him with it.

Depending on where you do the bathing, you might want to consider using a non-slip bath mat to help avoid any accidents. And remember, if your dog becomes frightened or upset, it's always better to back off and try again another day than force the issue.

When your dog is comfortable with this routine, you can add new elements to it such as tooth brushing and weighing. Depending on your dog, his fur, and living conditions, you may need to bathe him often or very rarely. Short-haired indoor dogs can do very well with infrequent baths and an occasional toweling down, whereas longer haired breeds need more attention. Whatever you do, you should try to brush his teeth at least weekly.

Refusing to be groomed and touched

It's possible that the problem isn't the water and bathtub at all, but that your dog simply refuses to have his paws, ears, tail, or belly touched in any way. As his human, you should have the ability to handle him for a number of reasons. Clipping his nails, brushing his coat, putting on a muzzle when needed, and checking for injuries are just a few of the ones that come to mind.

The solution for this is in many ways similar to the above explanation of how to introduce bathing. Your aim is to create a series of intermediary steps that your dog will find easier to accept so that you can reward and reinforce his patience and tolerance. If he can't stand the brush, begin by simply showing it to him and rewarding him. Once he can see you hold it without any sort of negative reaction, bring it closer to him and reward him for allowing you to do that. Eventually, work your way up to touching him lightly with the brush and rewarding him. Use as many intermediary steps as you need.

The same process applies to nail clippers with one distinction. Once your dog allows you to touch his nails with the clippers, you have to be extra careful in actually clipping the nail at the right height. If you go too far back, you will cut the quick of the nail, which is the sensitive living pink nerve at the center of it. Cutting the quick is extremely painful and it's a surefire way of making your dog never let you near him again.

If your dog refuses to allow you to touch him at all, regardless of whether you're holding a grooming implement or not, you need to start the process even further back and treat your hands like grooming tools.

A lot of dogs, if they aren't accustomed to it from a young age, will have a hard time letting you touch their face or paws. A good exercise in solving this issue is holding treats in one hand and lightly brushing against his body near the troublesome area with the other. Reward him for calm and steady behavior, but if he wiggles and pulls away, try again in an area that doesn't cause him discomfort. After each successful reward, move your hands, inch by inch, closer to the troubling zones. Don't rush the process if on the first day you only get down to his elbows rather than his paws, that's perfectly fine.

Be very careful only to offer rewards when he is calm and sitting still, and not if he's fidgeting and pulling away from you. This process can take a lot of patience, especially if your dog already decided he doesn't like to be touched, but it can be done over the course of multiple sessions and it is absolutely worth the trouble.

10.4 My dog is an escape artist!

Lots of adult dogs end up trying to escape the yard sooner or later. Sometimes it's because they're natural hunters and there's prey taunting them just outside. Sometimes it's because they smell a female in heat or because they're quite simply bored.

While it's almost impossible to guarantee that it'll never happen again – which is exactly why your dog should be microchipped – you can reduce his roaming desires in a number of ways.

The most important thing to do is to make sure that your dog is well exercised and stimulated. Take him for walks, teach him to play fetch or catch frisbees, teach him tricks, and give him the chance to hang out with other dogs. Physical and mental stimulation are crucial and often you can avoid 99% of problems by making sure you have a happy, tired dog.

If he has to be by himself, make sure he has entertainment. A nice chew toy or two, a few puzzle toys with food in them, a place to look out at the world, and a place to nap are often enough to keep a tired dog happy for many hours. Rotate his toys so that he doesn't get bored and make sure they are all safe for him to be left unsupervised with.

Finally, dog-proof your yard. Even the happiest dog might still decide to go roaming after a female in heat if you give him half the chance. Fences should be solid and buried half a meter deep, many breeds of dog being notorious diggers. Make sure to check the fences and gates regularly and don't underestimate the heights that a bored canine can reach by jumping or climbing!

10.5 Dog happiness and depression

Almost all dog owners reach a point where they begin to worry about the happiness and well-being of their dogs. Sometimes their behavior changes as a result of a change in their environment, and we wonder whether it might have had a more traumatic effect on our canine companion than we suspected. Things that seem small or natural to us, like moving into a different house, bringing home a baby, or the passing away of another pet, can all leave our dogs shaken.

Canine depression isn't actually that different from human depression. There are signs you can look out for and, usually, these are exactly the things which trigger worry in the first place.

1. Your energetic dog becomes listless. He's no longer interested in playing or going for walks. He spends most of his time staring out the window or into space.

2. He refuses to eat much.

3. He's not interested in his toys, chew bones, or in cuddles and affection.

4. He hides away somewhere where he wouldn't normally be spending time during the day.

5. He doesn't react to things that would normally stimulate him such as visitors, other dogs, the doorbell ringing, etc.

6. He trembles or drools more than would be normal for him.

Of course, many of these symptoms are also present whenever a dog has a medical condition or is in pain. If you have any doubts, your first course of action should always be to speak with your veterinarian and make sure there isn't a more pressing concern.

Once you have established that your dog is physically healthy, try to figure out what the cause of his depression might be. Here are some of the most common reasons why a pup would have the blues:

1. Changes in his environment

It's very common for dogs to feel down and out when moving away for example, or when major changes happen in the home. Even smaller things such as a family member changing schedules or a beloved friend no longer visiting can be enough.

2. Loss of a companion

Whether human or animal, the loss of a companion is not easy to deal with for pups. They create strong family bonds and often grieve for long periods when a member of their family passes away. Sometimes the grief can be attenuated by having other family members there for comfort, but for a dog that remains alone, the grieving period can be grueling.

3. Weather, seasons, and other changes

Pet moods can be impacted by the weather and the seasons as well. It's natural to slow down and become a little moody towards winter and to feel blue when we've had weeks of rain non-stop. Add to that the impossibility to play and exercise as much as they would like and you've got yourself a grumpy pup. There are also a lot of situations in which there is no specific reason that we can identify and we simply have to proceed to treat the symptoms.

10.6 How can we help treat depression in dogs?

Just like in humans, treating depression is not an overnight activity. There's no one thing that we can do to make everything better, but there are many small things we can do to make things a little less difficult. Here are some of the things you can look into, bearing in mind that if the situation doesn't show signs of improvement, however slow, you might need to consult with your vet and discuss the option of medication.

1. Sunshine and activities

Going out to enjoy the sun, fresh air, and nature is always good for us. Equally so for our canine friends who belong in nature more than we do! Take your dog out to the park, let him run around on the beach, or have him meet and hang out with other dogs. It might be just what he needs to get out of his bad mood. If you see him cheering up and enjoying his time outside, repeat as frequently as you can for the best results.

2. A good diet

You should always be feeding your dog the best possible diet you can afford. There's no reason to skimp on his food any more than you would on yours. However, particularly during a trying time, if you notice his appetite running low, don't be shy about springing for extra delicious and nutritious treats.

3. Vigorous exercise

If you can get your dog to be interested in something like a tug rope or a ball, you might have found the best cure for depression. A tired dog is a much less worried dog and therefore a much happier dog. Spending multiple sessions a day playing fetch is a great way to keep his spirits up and make it less likely that his depression will aggravate.

4. Love and patience

The most important resource you have is your love. It can take a long time for your pup to feel better and it certainly won't happen overnight, so your patience is crucial. Show him that you're there for him, spend time with him, and don't forget to take care of yourself as well. Whatever upset your dog is sure to have an impact on you too and a happy dog starts with a happy owner.

10.7 How can I tell if my dog is happy?

It makes sense that you want to know whether your dog is happy and satisfied with his life at any point, but even more so if he's just recovered from a traumatic event or period of depression. Here are some of the classic ways in which you can assess whether your dog is truly happy:

1. Body language and facial expressions

A happy dog has a relaxed face, usually keeps his mouth open and his brow smooth, and you can tell that his eyes are soft and ears are relaxed. His body will be loose, his tail up and wagging either quickly enough to shake his whole backside or with large, lazy wags. He will roll around on his back, tongue wagging.

2. Playful behavior

A happy dog is eager to play. He will play bow to you – lowering his front half to the ground with his backside high up in the air. You can tell that he's excited when you bring out the ball or the leash to go for a walk.

3. Contact

A happy dog will often come up to you and nudge you for attention or lean into you when you pet him. It's very likely that a happy dog would try to stay in close proximity to you as much as possible.

4. No destructive behavior

A happy, satisfied dog generally gets plenty of exercise and won't find himself bored or stressed often. That means that even if he's left home alone for some time, it's highly unlikely that he will chew up the furniture or destroy anything around the house. He shouldn't be chewing on his paws and tail either, as that would be a sign of serious anxiety.

11

COMMANDS EVERY ADULT DOG SHOULD KNOW

When you are training a puppy, that's a great time to experiment and try out every trick and game that you come across. Let's face it, most of us will! We see cool tricks at shows or see a video on youtube explaining how to high-five with your puppy and we will instantly try it ourselves. For a puppy, that's a wonderful and healthy way to interact! They are sponges for knowledge and, in the end, even the most pointless trick is still a happy fun time that you spent together.

However, when we are talking about an adult dog, we need to also draw the line and ask ourselves whether he knows the truly important commands that all adult dogs should know. It's not all about cute tricks and fun games. Some of these commands can be life-saving or at the very least are the foundation for much more important and complex activities.

One such example is when earlier we talked about replacing an aggressive behavior with a positive behavior such as sitting politely, going to his crate, or staying next to you. It won't be possible to enforce any of those behaviors without these basic building blocks. Let's take a look at what the absolute essential commands are and how we can teach our adult dog to obey them.

11.1 "Stop!"

Imagine these scenarios: It's a rainy, muddy day and you come home from an important meeting wearing your favorite suit. Your dog, having just played outside with the kids for an hour, is covered in mud and excited to see you. He starts running towards you.

Or perhaps you're taking the laundry up the stairs and are precariously balanced on the top step trying to pick up a fallen sock when you hear your dog galloping from around the corner.

Or perhaps you just dropped a piece of raw meat to the floor and watch as your dog is approaching it. In all of these situations, wouldn't it be nice to be able to shout "STOP!" and have him freeze, allowing you to take care of the situation before moving on?

It's not an easy thing to do, sure, and it takes work. But this is one of the most underused, undervalued and important commands in your arsenal. More than once "STOP!" has saved a dog from running right under a car. Here's what you need to do.

1. Set it up as a fun game. Remember when you were a kid and you would play "Red Light"? All the players start at the starting line and when you say "green light", they start running. If you say "red light", they must stop or be forced to return to the starting line. This is the same principle of teaching your dog the command "Stop" in a happy and playful way.

2. Make sure you have pocketfuls of treats before you begin and let him win a few by performing tricks he already knows or catching them out of the air. This is always a good start to a training session, just to let your dog know that you're going to play for a while, and there are prizes, and it will be good fun.

3. Start playing, jumping around and waving your limbs. Hopefully, this will get your dog excited and happy to play too. If you know any dance moves or tricks like "jump" or "spin", this is a good time to use them.

4. Suddenly say "STOP!" loudly and clearly. Freeze right where you are and don't move a muscle, not even your arms or eyes, not even if your dog bumps into you.

5. At first, your dog will probably keep moving around for a little bit. Eventually, concerned by the fact that you are unnaturally still, he should stop and investigate.

6. The moment he stops, even for a split second, say "Yes!" and reward him heavily. Make it a big party and go back to bouncing around and having fun.

7. Repeat steps three to six as needed. After many repetitions, you should notice that it takes your dog less and less time to stop. Once he understands that this is a game and that stopping is the goal, make him wait a little bit longer each time before giving him his reward. Don't make any dramatic increases, we're not aiming to go from one second to one minute in a single session.

8. Once you can say "STOP!" and have him stop moving reliably, it's time to increase the difficulty. Try doing it in a different place, on the street, or at the park. Try saying "STOP" and then moving one of his toys around. Take small, incremental steps so that you can immediately take a

step back if it becomes too much for him and he starts moving again.

9. Be very careful never to reward him unless he is motionless. If he is bouncing around and you give him the reward, you are reinforcing the wrong behavior and won't get any results.

11.2 "Drop it!"

Here's another useful command for you: whenever your dog has something in his mouth, be it food, or toy, or his own leash, and you want him to let go of it for you, you could use the command "Drop it!"

This is another amazing and potentially lifesaving command because if you practice it enough, you will reach a point where your dog will even be willing to drop scraps of food he picks up. This is especially important if you ever go hiking or even walking through the city because you never know what harmful things he might find on the ground and decide to taste. "Drop it" is not at all hard to teach and like all other important commands, it begins with a game.

1. Play tug. Tug of war is a highly educational game that you can use to teach a hundred different useful things. On top of that, it's a great workout and a wonderful bonding tool for you and your pup. You can use any sort of rag at first and graduate to a proper tug rope once your pup is confident and enjoys the game. While you are playing tug, keep the tug toy constantly moving. Motion is the key here, a toy in motion is interesting and one that sits still is boring.

2. After a minute of playing tug, grab hold of the toy firmly with both hands, pull it against your body in order

to make it impossible for your dog to move it any more, and sit perfectly still.

3. If you've done the previous exercise, you pretty much know what to expect now. Your dog will continue to move for a little big, yank on the toy, try to pull you down. Your job is to stay put and not move a muscle. Eventually, even if it takes a few minutes, your dog will get bored and release the toy.

4. When he releases the toy, say "Yes!" and immediately start playing again. This time, after a minute of play and motion, hold the toy very still against your legs and say "Drop it" and wait. No matter how much your dog pulls or whines or growls, do not move, do not let him steal the toy, and do not repeat the command. Try to avoid even laughing if you can.

5. As soon as he lets the toy go, say "YES!" and play again. Repeat this process hundreds of times and you will notice that your dog will eventually understand that "Drop it" means you want him to let go of the toy. He will become faster and faster at doing so. The one caveat is that you have to say the command once, then be firm and patient until he opens his mouth no matter how long it takes. If you move or repeat the command, you lose the game and have to start training again from the beginning.

6. Once your dog is truly comfortable dropping the toy – and if you've done the exercise right and he enjoys playing with you, you should see him absolutely spitting the toy out the moment you say "Drop it", happy to play by the rules – you can start to practice "drop it" with other things. In order to make the transition easy, start with other similar toys. Advance from his tug rope to a different rope, to a rag, to a soft frisbee, to a ball, to a squeaky toy, to a sock or shirt. Only allow him to put his mouth on "forbidden"

objects when you are absolutely certain that he will 100% drop them for you without question.

7. Once your dog is happy to drop all kinds of toys for you, try to graduate to food. Start slowly, maybe with a chew bone or unappetizing piece of bread. Work your way up to giving him a treat and then asking him to drop it – that is a real challenge that may take years to master.

8. For now, your dog is much more likely to drop something when you are holding it or, at the very least, when you are nearby. If you feel like that's getting too easy, try getting him to drop something when you are standing a few steps away!

11.3 "Look at me"

This command is a wonderful alternative when you're looking for something for your dog to do rather than react, bark, pull, or get agitated. One of the best things you can possibly do for those situations is training your dog that every time he sees a trigger – a squirrel, another dog, a cat – instead of reacting, he has to look at you.

It's very easy to teach the basics of this and you may very well begin to see results by the end of the day. The hard part is sticking with it and keeping it up in the long term since it can take a long time before your dog will be able to reliably perform this in an emergency situation.

1. Grab a very high-value treat. Make sure your dog knows you have it – and, while you're at it, make sure he's actually interested in it – and get him to sit patiently in front of you.

2. Give him a few rewards for sitting and staying still. Then, hold a treat up in front of your forehead, right between your eyes. Say "Look at me" and wait. Your dog

will naturally be looking at your face because that's where the treat is. Say "Yes!" and reward him. Repeat this step multiple times.

3. When it seems like he is starting to anticipate what you want, put treats in both hands. Bring one hand to your face, say "look at me" and, when he looks at your face, give him the treat that's in the other hand. This is to start teaching him that he won't always get the treat he's being shown.

4. When this goes smoothly, remove the treat from the hand that goes to your face instead, just using a finger to point to in between your eyes. Say "Look at me" and reward him when he does.

5. Work your way up over a few days in such a way that you don't need to raise your finger to your face each time and, instead, he responds to the verbal command alone. At this point, you should always be performing this exercise in a quiet, enclosed space, sitting as close to your dog as is comfortable.

6. When your dog responds to "look at me" without you needing to guide his eyes with your finger, take one step back and try this command again from a little further away. Remember to always reward the instant the correct behavior is produced and to reward heavily and happily, especially at the beginning.

7. Once you can say "look at me" from a few steps away and have your puppy look at you reliably, try doing it in a new place like outside or in a public space. One good trick is to sit somewhere reasonably far away from a school where your dog can still see the children but doesn't feel the need to go investigate them, and practice "look at me". Then, as he gets better at it, keep moving a little closer.

Increase the intensity of the distractions slowly and step back if it becomes too much.

11.4 "Leave it"

Leave it is another essential command. While "Drop it" tells your dog to spit out something he is holding in his mouth, "Leave it" tells him not to go get something that he wants. Usually, this is a fantastic command to have in case you drop something in the kitchen and don't want him to make a grab for it, or if you're trying to calm him down and stop him chasing the neighborhood cat.

Like all other commands, "Leave it" starts with a very simple game. However, you have to trust your dog not to injure you while you play this game, so if you know that you have a heavy biter or a dog who just isn't that delicate with his mouth – wear gloves.

1. Put a high-value treat in your hand. Make sure your dog sees it. Make a fist and let him try to open it up for a while to get at the treat. Do not, under any circumstances, let him win.

2. Eventually, even if it takes a very long time, your dog will get bored of trying to open up your hand and he will leave it alone. The moment he does that, praise him, open your hand, and give him the treat.

3. Put another treat into your fist and close it. Let him try to get at it for a while, then say "Leave it" and wait. When he leaves your fist alone, reward him and praise him.

4. Usually, most dogs will have understood the game by the tenth repetition and they will begin to leave your hand alone much faster as you say "leave it". When this happens, say "Yes" and reward them. Aim to get them to

perform the trick faster and faster, until there's almost no delay between you saying "leave it" and them leaving your hand alone.

5. Once this part is set, on the next round say "leave it", then start to slightly open up your fist. If your dog leaves it alone, as he should, even for just a split second, say "yes" and reward him. If he makes a go for the treat without you saying "yes", close your fist, calmly say "no", and tell him to "leave it" again.

6. Repeat this process several dozen times and aim to open your hand a little more each time. Your goal is to reach a point where you can have the treat on the open palm of your hand in front of your dog, but he doesn't try to grab it until you say "Yes!".

7. Be very careful that he never tricks you. If you tell him to "leave it" and he gets the treat anyway without your permission, you lose the game and have to start back at the beginning.

8. It can take many days before you can just place a treat in your palm, say "leave it" and wait. Once this happens, increase the difficulty by placing the treat on the ground, on his paw, on the chair. Practice it in as many ways as you can, as often as you can. And remember, never give him the chance to grab the treat before you say "yes" or you have to start the whole process again.

9. Once he becomes fairly good at this game, you can make it extra difficult by throwing the treat in his direction from a distance, or giving the command "leave it" and then throwing a ball or favorite toy. Whatever it is, make sure you increase the difficulty very very slowly and take a step back as soon as you notice it's getting a little too difficult for him to resist.

. . .

11.5 "Left" and "Right", "Up" and "Off"

Directions seem like a very complex thing for a dog to know and it's true, they aren't easy to teach. However, there are thousands of situations in day to day life where it helps to have the ability to tell your dog where to go, whether it's getting off the chair or up into the car, going left at the door or right towards the yard.

Note: We use "Off" rather than "Down" because "Down" already means something else – getting in a down position with his belly flat on the ground. If you use a different word for that position (Some people use "Lie"), then the choice of word is up to you.

No matter which direction you are teaching, the process is the same. Start by only teaching him directions one at a time, never having more than one per training session. Only when he is comfortable with them individually should you begin to mix them up in the same training session.

1. Grab some delicious treats. Use them to lure your dog, slowly and steadily, in the direction you are teaching – up on the chair or to his left, for example.

2. When your dog moves even a little bit in the right direction, say the command word - "Left" or "Up" - and reward him.

3. Repeat this process as many times as you can, taking incremental steps towards getting him to fully move in the direction that you want.

4. Once it seems like he is starting to understand the movement that you expect him to perform for that particular

word, you can remove the treat and simply gesture with your hand in order to get him to do the same action. The goal here is to eventually reach a point where you no longer have to gesture at all, or at most have to gesture only to indicate where specifically you'd like him to go.

5. In the case of left and right, you can make his reactions more precise by using a marker or traffic cone. Set the cone in the center of the room and lure your dog to the left or to the right of it, giving the appropriate command.

6. Another fantastic way to do this is to lure your dog slowly towards a wall in such a way that the only two choices are going left or right. Use treats to lure him in one direction, then give him the command word for that direction. In this case, it can be fun to switch it up between one and the other and see how long it takes before he is able to understand which direction you meant without using the lure at all.

11.6 "Heel"

Finally, the single most difficult command any dog absolutely needs to know is "Heel" or how to walk properly on a leash. There's no denying that most dog owners struggle greatly with this particular command and that it is necessary. All dogs need walks and knowing how to heel will just make things a lot nicer for both of you.

Bear in mind, however, that this technique will not teach you a competition heel – that is to say, the kind of formal, rigid "heel" where a dog is pressed to your leg, looks up at you, and moves only when you do. That kind of attention is incredibly hard to maintain and completely unnecessary outside of a formal contest situation – you want your dog to be a dog, to sniff and look around and enjoy his walk. Otherwise, why would you walk him at all?

An informal heel doesn't look as dramatic, but it's much more practical. It is a kind of "heel" where your dog will stay close to you, but not necessarily touching you. He will never be pulling on the leash, but he's welcome to look around and move within the boundaries of a relatively small circle around you.

So, how do we begin to teach this wonderful command? It couldn't be easier.

1. Slip on his harness and leash. Take him for a walk around the yard before you go out into the street.

2. Put a lot of good treats in your pocket. It also doesn't hurt to make sure he knows they're there at first.

3. Take a treat in your hand and, as you walk, let your hand drop by your side more or less where you would like the nose of your dog to be. If your treat is good enough, you can be sure that the nose will appear there shortly.

4. When your dog is in this correct position, say "Heel", then "Yes", and give him the treat.

5. Repeat this process multiple times. When you're comfortable doing this standing still, try doing it while walking.

6. Once you can do it while walking, work on increasing the time your dog has to stay in "Heel" before the treat is released. Do this by holding the treat in your hand in such a way that he can sniff it, but not get to it, and walking a few steps with him in the correct position. Don't push him to more than a few steps at first, as he could easily decide the treat isn't worth it and wander off.

7. Practice this process multiple times. Say "Heel" while walking and keep your hand with the treat where you would like his head to be. When he takes a few steps with you in the correct position, say "Yes" and reward him, aiming to make it a few more steps each time.

8. When you feel he is ready, finally take the show on the road and try this exercise on the street. Aim for a quiet street at first and then slowly increase the difficulty and intensity of the distractions.

With these basic commands, you already have a satisfying arsenal to turn to in case of any danger. Not only that, but all of these commands can be used to build more complex commands later on when you're ready to learn all the advanced tricks!

12

ACTIVITIES WITH YOUR ADULT DOG AND HOW TO DO THEM SAFELY

There are few things in life nicer for a dog lover than doing some sort of fun activity with his canine friend. Whether it's jogging, water fetch, camping, or dog sports, there's something out there for everyone.

Before we begin, it's a good idea to mention that a basic first aid course for yourself and your dog is a bare minimum for anyone interested in doing anything more dangerous than walking. Even if you plan on having a couch potato dog, knowing their basic anatomy and what you should do in case of an emergency is common sense. Talk to your vet or local training center to organize a lesson, or at the very least take one of the numerous certified online courses. Learn what to do in case of drowning, burns, cuts, broken bones, breathing problems, and unconsciousness at the very least. Wherever you go with your dog, especially if engaging in sports or leisure activities, make sure you know where the nearest non-stop emergency service for animals is and how to reach them.

Let's take a look at the most popular choices of human-canine activities available for amateurs and consider what steps we need to take in order to keep ourselves and our furry friends safe.

12.1 Jogging or cycling with your dog

One of the many reasons to welcome a high-energy dog into your life is if you want company while you strive to reach your fitness goals. Many people turn to jogging with their dogs. It's a fun activity that allows you both to get the exercise you need and strengthens your bond, as well as being easy to pick up and not needing a lot of special equipment beyond a pair of running shoes.

Naturally, before jogging with your dog, you must be able to walk with him. A tolerable "heel" is the very least you should have in your arsenal. Getting dragged around at high speed by an over excited husky is the last thing you need.

Be aware that running together will raise his level of energy and excitement, so if you already have a dog who likes to zip around everywhere and just can't seem to calm down, running together could potentially be a dangerous thing to do. Only try this if you are reasonably confident that you can keep your dog calm and collected.

The one tool you could consider getting aside from a good pair of running shoes is a leash with a bit of elasticity that you can clip to your belt. It's nice to have your hands free while running and the elasticity means there will be less jolting if you need to suddenly stop and your dog keeps going.

Be sure to carry water with you, both for yourself and your dog. The only other major concern is road safety: don't go jogging anywhere where a sudden turn to the left or right could put him in danger of ending up under a car. If you act as though you expect him to dash after a squirrel at all times, even if he never does, you will be fine.

It helps if your dog has some rough idea of the commands "left" and "right", but you can do without those if he is calm and has a good "heel".

Biking with your dog is a whole other level of difficulty. This activity could potentially be very dangerous and you shouldn't engage in it without the proper preparation first. The problem here is that an overly excited or overly frightened dog could easily either pull you off your bike, pull you into traffic, or jump under your bike wheels. These are all things we want to avoid, so you should prepare for this activity with great care.

The first step is to get an extension rod that attaches your dog's leash to the bike but helps keep it away from the bike itself so as not to get it tangled in the wheels or pedals. Spend some time on a quiet side street just walking with your dog attached to your bike, without getting on the bike itself, and get him used to the sound and look of this massive metal object next to him.

You should only move to the next step when you're absolutely certain that he is comfortable with this one. Sticking to side streets only, start to get on your bike but moving still at a steady walking pace. Do not accelerate and do not go on roads with traffic on them. If you see another pedestrian, dog, bike, or car approach you, dismount immediately and walk normally.

You should spend many days taking your dog on quiet walks in this way, alternating between walking next to your bike and riding on it very slowly at a walking pace. Do not ever allow your dog to pull the bike. It may seem like fun at first, but this can become very dangerous very quickly. If he does pull, be sure to hit the brakes immediately, stop completely, and get him back into a heel position. He should, over time, learn that if he tries to pull, the fun stops. This has to happen immediately and consistently, otherwise, it won't work.

Yes, there are people who have their bikes pulled by dogs through the woods. These are professional sportsmen and this isn't something you should try without proper training.

Slowly increase the speed at which you ride. The moment he breaks into a run, your dog will be tempted to speed off and go faster than you. If you allow this to happen now, you will have a very hard time keeping control of him later, so no matter how frustrating it is, stop him every single time and get him back into the heel position. Pick one side of the bike he should be on and never allow him to move from that side, this is very important. If he ever makes any sudden or random moves, stop. If he pulls, stop. If he seems scared or unhappy in any way, stop.

If it looks like your dog is having fun, can stay in heel without any issue, and doesn't mind going at your speed, congratulations. You now have a wonderful way to exercise both yourself and your high-energy dog.

One other thing you should keep in mind is that safety is paramount for both you and your dog. Wear a helmet, knee and elbow pads at the very least. Make sure he is wearing a proper sports harness and under no circumstances do this while he's attached by a collar. If at any point you feel unsafe, it's better to stop and try a different sport.

12.2 Water sports

Some dogs are designed to be in the water. Dogs like the Golden Retriever are likely to never be happier than when they're chasing a stick into a muddy lake. Even the breeds that aren't designed for it can absolutely have a wonderful time and love playing in the water, as long as you introduce it to them in the right way.

Most dogs will, at first, be skittish about water, especially moving water. The motion and the noise can be quite intimidating, which is why it's best to begin the introductions with a nice still pool that isn't too hot or too cold. One fantastic way to acclimate your dog to water is by simply using a kiddie pool in the back yard. It's a great way to cool off in the summer and can cost under $20 on Amazon.

You should never introduce your dog to water by force. Carrying them into the sea or pointing a hose at them is a quick way to get them to hate water and never trust you again. Instead, let them spend as much time around it as they like without any sort of pressure on your part. Play around it, especially high energy games like tug or fetch.

Eventually, if he's not interested in investigating the water on his own, you can consider throwing a toy near or in the water, or tossing a treat in there for him. Make sure he has a clear and easy way in and out of the pool so that he doesn't have to panic and scramble out. If he's not willing to go in, do not push. Start with a shallower pool or even just a plastic tub filled with water up to ankle-height.

Lots of terrier breeds are going to enjoy "digging" into such a pool of water, so a setup like this one could easily end up saving you a lot of holes in your garden.

All dogs can swim. It's not your job at all to teach him how to do that, he will know it by instinct and do it in the best way for him. Your only job is to make sure he's introduced to the idea slowly and doesn't develop any fear of water.

Once you see your dog swimming around happily in still water, you can add extra challenges such as a hose, a sprinkler, or going to a body of water that has waves and motion. If your dog is happy to swim – great! Time to break out the toys.

One of the absolute best ways to get a dog happy and exhausted is to play fetch in a body of water. You may have to start by throwing the stick or toy only a very short distance, where he can retrieve it without even swimming, just to get him used to the idea. Be sure to pick a highly visible toy that floats!

It is still advisable, even in this situation, to have your dog wear a harness and have him attached to a long, 30-60 foot (10-20 meter) lead so that you can get him out of trouble in case of an emergency and impose just how far away from you he is allowed to swim. In case of any choppy or dangerous waters, you should absolutely have a doggie life jacket, but that's only something you should do after you've extensively practiced swimming in normal waters.

Before doing any of this, however, be sure that you know, at the very least, how to perform CPR on your dog.

12.3 Camping with your dog

One of the absolute most fun and exciting things to do is go camping with your dog. This activity includes a lot of other fun things such as hiking, swimming, exploring, nose work, and many others. Before you begin, there are a few things you have to ask yourself.

1. Does your dog know basic commands? At the very least,

he should respond consistently to sit, stay, and heel. He must absolutely come when called. If this isn't something you have down yet, practice more before going camping.

2. Do you have the right equipment? Is your tent big enough? Is your car? Do you have a secure travel crate for your dog? Do you have a way to keep him warm? Will he be sleeping in the tent with you? Do you have a sturdy leash? Do you need a backup?

3. Do you have activities planned? If you intend to pitch a tent and sit still enjoying nature for three days, that might not be ideal. There's nothing wrong with it, but your dog might expect a little more.

Prepare your dog for camping trips by taking shorter, day trips to nearby parks and woods first. Let him see what it's like to sniff about and get the scent of wild animals. Especially for hunting breeds, the scent of squirrels can be very exciting and might easily make them forget whatever they were trained to do.

Practice your basic commands outdoors often, especially coming when called. Practice them around small children and other animals. It would be very useful to be able to recall your dog even if he sees a squirrel dashing through the forest.

Before you leave, make sure that your dog is microchipped, that the information on the microchip is correct, and that he has all the necessary vaccinations for the area you'll be visiting. You should also have flea and tick protection in place. A collar with a tag containing your name and phone number isn't mandatory since your dog is microchipped, but it might still be a good idea as it can provide a faster way to track you down if anyone finds your potentially lost dog. A highly reflective harness is also a great idea.

If you feel reasonably confident with your arsenal of commands and tools, it's time to pack everything up and pick a place to visit. Pick a nice, quiet campsite in nature that isn't highly trafficked. Many strange dogs and people might sound like fun at first, but this is already a strange and stressful experience and there's no need to add to the stress by introducing too many strangers. If you can, go together with friends that already know your dog and whom he is happy to spend time with. Otherwise, go alone.

Once you've picked a place, make sure you know what their dog policies are and if there are any extra costs to bringing a dog with you. Some campsites will charge you, others won't, while free camping usually means you're welcome to bring your dog as long as you keep everything clean and neat just as you do after yourself.

One of the best things about camping with your dog, aside from the help in keeping warm at night, is the fact that you can do all sorts of fun things together out in nature. Here are some ideas for fun activities for both of you:

1. Hiking – Few things are as enjoyable for your dog as a good hike around unknown grounds. He gets to smell all sorts of new things, mark brand new trees, and get a good workout out of it. A nice long leash and comfortable harness will keep things relaxed for both of you. While many people choose to let their dog off-leash in the forest, this is actually a terrible idea. Wild animals could pose a potential danger, especially if you have a hunting breed that's likely to rush off at any moment. A long lead is plenty for him to enjoy his freedom without putting himself in danger.

2. Nose games – Most dogs will be good at tracking scents to some degree or another. While they're not all blood-hounds, sniffing around and looking for treats is still a

fantastic exercise and will engage their brain in a way that is more satisfying and tiring than the longest game of fetch. Try dragging a favorite toy or bone across the path and hiding it in the leaves somewhere nearby, then sending them off to look for it. Make it very easy to find at first and you'll see how quickly your dog falls in love with this game. Soon, you will be able to walk away for a good distance and hide a treat, and your dog will be able to track it by your scent alone. Just be sure that you leave him with someone he's comfortable with.

3. Water sports – we've discussed this at length above, but it bears repeating here because camping is the perfect situation in which you might have access to a river or lake nearby. Playing fetch with a nice bright frisbee in the water is a wonderful exercise and, even if you don't have a large body of water nearby, sploshing around and chasing fish in a stream is still fun and relaxing.

5. Hide and seek – a more advanced version of nose game, this is potentially great fun for both of you. Have someone hold your dog while you walk away. Let him see where you're going at first. Hide behind a tree, make it very easy for him to find you, and call him to you. Have a treat ready for him when he finds you and reward him. Next time, walk away behind him so that he doesn't see where you went. If he enjoys this game, you can go further and further away and hide each time. Eventually, you can let him find you by nose alone, without ever calling him to you.

13

FINAL THOUGHTS ON BEING A GOOD DOG OWNER

Having a dog in your life is a huge responsibility. It takes time, money, and the willingness to learn with and from your dog. It's not something that should be done lightly, no more than having a child should be done lightly. You are responsible for another life and it will change the way you live yours completely.

It can also be a harrowing experience. Many beginner owners struggle. There's such a thing called "puppy blues" or "post-puppy depression" where new and even experienced dog owners get a puppy and then immediately regret that decision for the next four to twelve weeks. There's also the adolescent phase in which we get to regret that decision all over again. Many people struggle because they didn't expect exactly how much attention a dog would need.

There's also the issue of the breed. If you don't know much about breeds, you might want to pick a dog because he's cute and playful, or because you've seen them on TV. That's how people end up with Border Collies or even the fearsome Jack Russell Terrier. One month later, he ate your couch and your neighbors hate you, and you don't know what to do.

Being overwhelmed or even panicked about your dog is normal. This is a perfect time to seek professional help. There's no shame in admitting that you bit off more than you could chew, were unprepared for the task, and need help. The fact that you're willing to stick with it through the hard times and learn how to do better is a testament to your goodwill, and nobody has any right to tell you otherwise. Having a dog is hard. You have the right to complain and to make mistakes. Doing your best and being able to learn is what counts.

Many trainers and professionals out there think it's ok to scold or chide a dog owner who didn't know what he was doing and made bad decisions. Thank these trainers for their opinion and go look for a new one. You should no more accept that kind of behavior from a dog trainer than you would from a therapist you went to seeking help.

Whatever else happens, as long as you always have the best interest of your dog at heart and are able to be calm and patient with him, you will be rewarded. It gets so much easier after the first year that you won't even remember how hard it used to be, and might even make the decision to get a second puppy.

This being said, once you settle into a rhythm and understanding with your dog, it is absolutely one of the most amazing experiences in the world. Nothing compares to the satisfaction of seeing that happy face greet you as soon as you get home. Performing tricks for your friends is one of the most fun things in the world and you will always have a loving companion no matter what adventures you decide to have. If you are willing to put in the work and the time, you will never be able to go back to living without dogs in your life. They enrich every single aspect of our existence and never fail to make us, in many ways, better people than we were before we had them.

PART III

BONUS TIPS

14

TEACH YOUR DOG TO STOP BARKING

Excessive, unwanted barking is one of the main reasons why dogs are returned to shelters. That's a terrible shame because in almost every instance barking is a manageable problem with a little patience and education. If you want to save yourself a lot of trouble, headaches, and complaints from the neighbors, keep reading!

Tips before you start

Keep in mind that you have to approach this activity with total calm every single time. If you are absolutely sick and tired of your dog barking at the door, that is the wrong time to start training. Your job is to be a tranquil, assertive, kind, a leader and an educator, so you have to be in a good state of mind before moving forward.

Resist the temptation to use any tricks, the well-intended advice of neighbors, or any aggressive deterrents. Things like spray bottles or shock collars are terrible ideas – not only will they not get you the results that you want, they will train your dog to be fearful, reactive, and potentially aggressive. The only safe way to educate a dog is through positive, upbeat training.

Finally, be sure that your dog learns the same thing, consistently, from every member of the family. It's not enough that you enforce certain rules – if the rules go out the window the moment you leave the room, you'll never get rid of self-rewarding behaviors like barking.

Step one – when does your dog bark?

The first thing you need to do is identify when exactly the problem occurs. No dog barks 100% of the time, and most of them bark for the same reasons. Here are some of the most common situations that cause excessive barking:

- The doorbell rings

- Someone passes by the house

- Strangers, cats, cars, or other interesting things pass within view or earshot

- Mail is delivered

- Your dog wants something from you

- Your dog is left alone for a long period of time

While you are training your dog, make sure that whatever stimuli you've identified doesn't happen, or happens as little as possible if you can't stop it. It won't be an instant process, and you will have to train him to keep his cool in baby steps, so getting triggered over and over again will make that process impossible.

Step two – a tired dog is a happy dog

And a happy dog is much more likely to be a quiet dog. Like many other problems, barking can be greatly reduced by making sure that your dog is physically and mentally tired every day. He may ignore smaller stimuli altogether if he's already tired, and even stronger ones like the mailman won't have as much appeal.

We've covered options on getting your dog tired elsewhere in this book, but long walks and good games of tug and fetch as well as obedience and trick training are your best bets. Make sure you do something extra interesting like visiting new places or trying new sports at least once a week and make sure your dog plays both with people and other dogs. This should already go a long way towards helping your situation.

Step three – prevention is better than the cure

Once your dog starts barking there are few things you can do. The trick is to work with him before he's exposed to the stimulus and prepare him. There are two things you can do before the barking ever begins.

1. Desensitize

If your dog reacts particularly strongly to a certain sound or view, start exposing them to a version of that from a great distance. Record the sound on your phone and play it very quietly, or watch a cat pass by from very far away – or even on TV. The further removed your dog is from the stimulus, the easier it will be for him to resist the temptation to bark.

If he is quiet, reward him and move a little closer. If he seems like he might bark, try doing a quick fun trick like "shake" or "roll over" and reward him heavily when he performs it. If he's refusing to obey you and starts barking, say "no" calmly, and move even further back until he's able to work with you again.

Find that ideal distance or intensity of stimulus where he's not tempted to react and play with him and reward him there, slowly moving closer to the stimulus only when you're confident that he can handle it. Reduce the distance over a period of weeks and you'll see great results.

2. Teach him the "shh" command

If your dog already has a good grasp of "no" and "yes", practice the "shh" command with him when you're playing. Dogs will often give out one or two barks during playtime. When he does, calmly say "no" and "shhh" with a treat in your hand.

It's very likely that the strange sound combined with the treat will get him to stop and sniff your hand. When he does, say "yes" and reward him. Do this many times, and after a few hundred repetitions you'll notice that your dog will respond more quickly to the "shh" command.

This isn't going to be a magic button – when he's incredibly excited by a passing cat, for example, no amount of shushing will stop him from barking. But if you combine this trick with a tired dog as well as desensitizing him to his most common stimuli, odds are you'll be able to bring the barking to a manageable level.

Step four – what to do when he's already barking

It happens, you're caught off guard, the mail-man came at a strange time, and your dog is in full-on barking mode. You know it's unlikely he will stop for many minutes. Barking is terrible because it's self-rewarding, the more he does it the more he will enjoy doing it in the future. Here are a few things you can do:

1. Crate time. If your dog enjoys his crate, take him there as soon as he starts barking and leave him inside with a treat. Close the door between him and the problem, and

don't let him come back out again until it's gone and the barking stops.

2. Incompatible behavior. If your dog is barking, try getting him to do some other activity that just isn't compatible. Pull out a nice toy stuffed with peanut butter that he goes crazy for and ask him to sit, shake, or do any trick at all for you. If he does the trick, reward him with the treat that will keep him nice and busy for a long time.

3. Distance. Most of the time he's going to bark because he wants to get at something – the intruder, the cat, the ice-cream truck. Snap a leash on him and take him on a walk as far away as you possibly can from what he wants, so that he doesn't feel rewarded for his behavior, then begin desensitizing him.

Step five – treating attention barking

The one kind of bark that doesn't rely on an external stimulus is attention barking. That's what happens when your dog wants something from you, be it food, cuddles or just attention, and he learned that if he annoys you for long enough you will give it to him.

This can happen because your dog is reaction barking and you respond to it by giving him attention or treats. Obviously, in this case, the first step to curing it is replacing your reaction with one of the solutions we've detailed above.

Once you've started making a positive impact on reaction barking, you have to also deal with attention barking. Unsurprisingly, the best solution for this is to completely ignore it. You will have to be very patient and stubborn, because giving in at all will simply teach your dog that he needs to bark more in order to get what he wants.

In order to help you remember what you need to do, try

pretending that whenever your dog is barking at you, he's invisible. Don't even look at him! Look up at the sky, look away, don't talk to him. Pretend like he doesn't exist.

When he eventually gets tired and stops barking at you, count five seconds and reward him with a treat. Doing this over a long period of time will reduce attention-seeking behavior and teach him that barking is not the right way to get what he wants.

15

BOARDING YOUR DOG - THINGS
TO KNOW

Sometimes it's just not possible to take your beloved Ace with you on vacation. Often times, if flights are involved, bringing him could be costly and very uncomfortable for everyone. The best thing to do in these situations is find someone who can take care of him and ensure that he gets a vacation of his own – luckily, dog boarding is a booming business and the answer to all of your needs.

You have a couple of options when it comes to having someone keep your dog for an extended stay: either find friends or family who are happy to do it or trust a professional. The advantage of having your family do it is that you already know them and their house, and the dog is probably already very comfortable with them. He may have already visited them many times, and moving there for a while won't be as great a shock. The advantage with a professional is that they will have more experience in dealing with dogs, especially if they have behavior issues, need special attention or require medication. Unlike a family member who needs to go on with their normal life, a professional will spend their entire time with the dogs they are boarding.

As far as professional boarding is concerned, you have the option of finding a kennel or an at-home sitter. Depending on where you live, one or the other may not be available. A kennel will be cheaper, but won't be nearly as comfortable for your dog and isn't always ideal for long stays.

Before you board

Check the reviews for your sitter or kennel carefully. Be sure you're leaving your dog in good hands, and if you can avoid it, don't use a service that has no credentials at all.

If your dog is staying in an unfamiliar place, make sure you visit it together at least once. Take a tour, see where he will sleep and spend their time, and let him sniff around. This will give you some peace of mind and will make your dog more comfortable when you leave him there.

Make sure your dog is ready. He has to have all his vaccinations and paperwork in order, and you need to provide him with absolutely everything he might need during his stay – his bed or blanket, his food, his medicine, his favorite toy, his leash and collar, and his crate.

Inform the people responsible for your dog of any special needs. Make sure they have your contact, a backup contact, and the phone number of your veterinarian as well as a 24-hour clinic nearby.

Find out what you can expect in terms of being informed on your dog's daily activities. In general, kennels won't update you, but many private dog-sitters will be happy to send you daily messages or photos to check in. If you're nervous about leaving your dog with someone else, this can be the single greatest cure.

When you drop off your pet, make sure you don't forget anything and don't take a long time to say goodbye. Making a fuss is only going to cause them more stress. Leave as though you're going to the store on any normal day, and save the cuddles for when you get back.

When you return

Pick your pet up on time and make sure you take all of their things with you. Double-check that you have their paperwork.

Ask about any problems and thank your host for taking care of your pet. As much as you'd love to spend the whole time showering your pup with kisses, their human host deserves your gratitude! If there are any problems, be patient and understanding and do your best to resolve them calmly.

Keep in mind that being away from you is stressful for your dog no matter where he stays, so there's a good chance his behavior might seem odd in the first few days after you pick him up. Here are some of the things you can expect which are perfectly normal:

- He seems exhausted and sleeps all the time

- He seems extremely hyperactive and never sleeps

- He eats a lot more

- He eats a lot less

- He sniffs around the house a lot

- He has potty accidents

- He insists on staying close to you all the time

- He never comes near you and wants to be alone

All of these behaviors, while odd for your dog, can happen after boarding and shouldn't worry you. You can expect them to pass within a few days. There are, however, situations in which you could be rightfully concerned:

- If your dog is still acting strangely a week after being returned home

- If your dog is aggressive or angry

- If he completely refuses to eat or drink

- If he coughs, limps, has any odd scrapes or bumps, or shows any other sign of illness

- If he has ticks of fleas

In any of these situations, you'll want to talk both to your kennel to understand the possible causes, and to your veterinarian to check your dog's health and offer you solutions.

Final tips

If you are nervous about leaving your dog alone or if it's your first time doing so, consider doing a trial run. Arrange for them to stay at your chosen kennel for one night, just so both of you can get used to the idea.

If you decide to leave him with friends or family instead, remember that no matter how much they care about him, it's still a commitment. They will be responsible for his safety and will have to make their plans around him. A token of gratitude, especially if you want to ask for their help in the future, is the least you can do. If they won't accept some payment, offer to babysit or help them in other ways.

Finally, remember that no matter what you do, no

boarding situation will be perfect. Your dog hates being away from you as much as you hate being away from him, but sometimes it's necessary. Be patient and understanding, keep calm, and both of you will soon recover from having been apart!

16

FUN THINGS TO DO WITH YOUR DOG

16.1 A safe improvised agility course

Playtime with your dog can be one of the most pleasant moments of the day for both of you, no matter what you're doing. If you have an active breed or a young dog, energetic games and sports are going to be a part of your daily life for a very long time. Both your health and that of your pup will benefit greatly, and it will help strengthen the bond between you. Not to mention the fact that a tired dog is a happy dog!

There are many things that you can do together, but few are as effective as an agility course – especially for high-energy terrier and shepherd breeds. These kinds of games may not be ideal for older dogs, very young pups who are not done growing yet, or dogs with short snouts who have a harder time breathing.

Naturally, if you want to participate in official agility competitions, you will want to practice on a formal standard course by going to a licensed training facility – otherwise, your dog will learn all the wrong jumps and moves.

But if you only want to use it as a fun activity, there's no reason why you can't improvise many of the obstacles at home.

Your number one priority has to always be safety. Never use any obstacle that isn't 100% safe for you and your dog, and always err on the side of caution. Obstacles which have moving parts, such as the see-saw, should be avoided altogether; high boardwalks or high jumps are also not recommended. One of the great things about an improvised agility course is that you don't need any high jumps or spectacular tools – the simpler and easier obstacles also happen to be the most fun for your dog, and are easy to set up.

Start and stop platforms

A good thing to start with is a starting platform. This can be something as simple as a pillow or a piece of cardboard on the floor – make sure it doesn't slip and slide, use tape if necessary – or it can be a raised platform such as a chair or a cushioned wooden box. Whatever it is, make sure that it's safe and doesn't wobble, and that your dog has plenty of space to jump up on it comfortably.

The point of the platform is to give your dog a place to start from, a place to rest in between obstacles, and a place to finish the course on. It seems simple, but think of it like an athlete's starting line and finish line – it helps to concentrate the mind and it gives a lot of satisfaction knowing you've successfully completed a course.

Since your dog knows "sit" and "stay", get him to perform these on his starting platform a few times to get ready. Then, whenever you do any of the tricks, start by having them sit on their platform. Give them the ok to come away from it and do the exercise, then return to it when you are done and reward him for sitting.

16.2 The slalom

The slalom is a great challenge for your pup's mind and body. It's a very safe obstacle because it doesn't involve any jumps or climbs, and it's one of the most difficult and rewarding exercises you can teach him.

Before attempting this, try some of the previous tricks we've taught you. In order to go through a slalom, ideally, your dog should be used to following a treat lure comfortably, and in order to make your job easier, he should also know "sit" and "stay".

You will need six to twelve straight poles, either made of plastic, PVC, or wood, and a way to keep them upright. While official agility slalom poles move from side to side, this isn't strictly necessary in order to create a fun obstacle for your dog.

One good and durable way to source these is from any sports equipment store that stocks soccer training cones and poles. They tend to be lightweight, durable, and easy to move around and set up.

Otherwise, any PVC pipe or even sticks stuck in the ground will do. Just make sure that everything is smooth and there are no sharp, pointy edges that might hurt you or your dog.

For a very cheap and very safe slalom, don't throw away your plastic water bottles! Keep them until you reach a good number, then fill them with water and place them in a slalom pattern. Even if your dog knocks into them, he won't get injured.

In order to start teaching your dog to navigate the slalom, find a clear area of your yard or a good-sized space indoors – this can potentially make a great rainy day activity. Place your bottles, cones, or other obstacles in a row with plenty of space between them – you have to be able to pass through comfortably without needing to corner too sharply. Your dog is likely not going to be very good at this, at first, so you can expect him to knock everything around a lot. Make sure there's no way he can injure himself, so remove anything that might break, and tighten the lids of your water bottles as much as you can.

Step One

If your dog is comfortable following a lure in your hand, walking by your side in a straight line, do that now a few times in order to show him what your expectations are with this exercise. Pick one side – ideally, the same one he's used to when he walks on a leash with you – and stick to it throughout your agility training; that way, it will be easier to guide your dog and you'll avoid confusions.

Contrary to appearances, an agility course isn't a frantic, quick exercise. You need to start slowly and build up speed as you get better at it. Maintain an attitude of calm and relaxation throughout the entire thing. Performing these tricks tends to get most dogs excited and the calmer you stay to balance it out, the better.

Reward him whenever he confidently and calmly follows the lure and walks where you guide him. After you've had your dog walk by your side in a straight line following a treat in your hand a few times, it's time to attempt the first steps of the slalom.

Step Two

Start with only two obstacles – in this example, let's use the safe and easy plastic bottles filled with water. Before you start the slalom, pick a starting direction. Do you want your dog to go around the very first bottle on the right side or on the left? Make a decision and be sure to always start in the exact same way. Dogs like structure and habits and learn much faster if you keep things constant.

Get your pup on his starting platform, then have him rest there for thirty seconds. Come away from it and guide him slowly – at about half the pace of your normal walk – with a treat in your hand. Use your hand like a magnet to guide their nose. Go around the first bottle remembering to always do it in the same direction. Then pass in between the two bottles and around the second one. Once he's passed the second bottle, reward and repeat!

Step three

Once your dog is comfortable following your hand through two bottles, add a third and even a fourth. If it becomes too much and he gets lost or confused, take it back one step and guide him more slowly. Repeat whatever he's comfortable with many times before adding an extra step.

Eventually, after hundreds of repetitions, you will start to notice that your dog happily passes through the first few bottles by himself, now knowing exactly what you expect him to do. When that happens, you can start to remove the lure and add more bottles, the goal being to get him to eventually complete a twelve-bottle course by himself. How long that will take depends on your pup, but if you are patient and persevere you can do it!

16.3 Jumps

The one thing most people, kids especially, love to see a dog do is to perform a beautiful jump over an obstacle.

A note on jumps: since you're just trying to have fun with your dog, your number one priority has to be his health and safety. Do not attempt to make him do extremely high jumps, to jump over great distances, or jumping in general until you're certain he is fully grown and his bones have finished developing. If he seems in any way reluctant or uncomfortable, take a step back, lower the height, make it easy for him, or stop altogether.

If you don't want to purchase jump obstacles from the pet store or sports store, you can make your own with light-weight PVC pipes, or even improvise by using cardboard, rope, or light plastic tubes set across objects like bricks, buckets or chairs. There are two rules when making a jumping obstacle: make sure that the landing on the far side is absolutely clear and safe, and make sure that they're made out of a light material that your dog can easily knock into without injuring himself. Assume that sooner or later, your dog will fail the jump and tumble into the obstacle at full-speed. If that happens, could he get injured? Good obstacles fall apart at the slightest touch so that you can see whether your dog cleared them properly but it won't hurt his toes if he hits them.

One of our personal favorites is simple: take a light plastic broom handle and lay it across two bricks. First, lay the bricks down so that it's barely a few inches off the ground. That's the kind of height you want to begin with so that your dog can easily step over it without any effort. He has to learn what you expect him to do before actually jumping.

Step one

Set up your jump low enough that your dog can step over it. Have him "sit" and "stay" on his starting mat, ideally lined up in front of the jump with a lot of clearance between the two. Give him a good three or four steps before and after the jump which are clear of any obstacles.

With your dog staying on his starting mat, place yourself on the other side of the jump, off to the side so that he doesn't bump into you. With a treat in your hand, call him to you. At first, he will come over, stepping over the obstacle easily, barely noticing it's there at all. That's ideal. When he comes to you, reward him. If, for some reason, he goes around the obstacle, don't reward him. Calmly lead him back to the starting mat and try again, either with a lower obstacle or by positioning yourself closer to it.

Step two

Once your dog passes over the obstacle a few times, raise the height – set the bricks upright, or exchange them for buckets or anything else. The ideal height now is one where your dog cannot pass underneath the obstacle yet, but only has to make a very small jump to get over it. If he struggles at any point, lower the bar again.

Position yourself and the dog in the same way as before, and call him over. Ideally, he will hop over the low obstacle and you can reward him. Repeat this phase a few times. Once he does it comfortably, feel free to raise the jump higher, but remember – you're only doing this for fun. Don't push him to the limit. Your jumps should never be higher than he would comfortably jump when chasing a ball or to catch a fly. Trust him to know what he's comfortable with.

Step three

Rather than raise the difficulty with higher jumps which

can put unnecessary strain on his legs and spine, do it by setting up two or three consecutive jumps, or by mixing up jumps with the slalom and with pauses on the mat. Combining multiples of these three elements in creative ways is all you need to have a fun and engaging agility course for your dog!

17

POTENTIAL SOURCES OF INCOME

So you've had a dog – or multiple dogs – for a while and you're considering using your skills and knowledge to make some extra money. That's wonderful! There are plenty of ways you can help your local community and earn some extra cash if you're good with dogs; and if you've followed all of our instructions and practised, there's no reason why you shouldn't be.

First of all, remember that not all dogs are like your dog. In fact, most other dogs will feel completely different and react in ways you can't even anticipate. A great way to start getting a feel for what it's like to work with other dogs is to volunteer at your local shelter.

Many shelters will let you help out, or even let you take the dogs out on walks. They will tell you about the way each dog behaves and what you can expect from them, and you'll have a chance to deal with a wide array of problems like leash pulling or chasing. As long as you're careful and respect what the shelter employees tell you, you'll do fine!

Once you have some experience working with dogs other than your own, consider volunteering to dog-sit for your friends and family. This can still be a difficult task and you need to be careful, but it is a good way to work up to dog-sitting for money. Plus, it means that once you start charging, you can already say that you have some experience doing it.

Another great way to work with new dogs is to volunteer as a foster home for dogs. This is a much more complex and involved process and you shouldn't embark on it lightly. It involves hosting one or more dogs at your house until such a time as they are adopted by their forever families. If this sounds like something you might be interested in doing, your local shelter or foster association can help you get started.

Dog walking for fun and profit

If you enjoy taking walks and live in an area where there are lots of pet owners, then maybe dog-walking is the right choice for you. With minimal supplies and a little preparation, you can make money doing something that's also very healthy for you.

What do you need in order to become a dog walker?

1. You need to have a flexible schedule. Most owners will need you to work around their work hours and take the dogs out at specific times. If you already have a full-time job, it will be hard to find any clients at all that fit in the same time frame you have available. It's not impossible, but it will be rare and won't make you much money.

2. A little experience with dogs. If you've followed our

guidance and taught your own dog how to walk on a leash, how to behave and even a few tricks, you know more than enough about how to handle professional dog walking. Just be sure to listen very carefully to the owners and what they tell you about their dogs.

3. A lot of patience. You may be working with dogs that don't get out much, or dogs that are completely uneducated. They may have strange fears and odd behaviors. It's your responsibility to be patient, keep them happy and safe, and teach them how to be comfortable walking on a leash.

4. Digital skills. It may seem like a strange thing, but the truth is that nowadays most freelancing jobs – dog walking among them – happen through apps and websites. Depending on where you live, there's probably a local app such as "Wag!" that connects walkers to customers. You can always go the old-fashioned route and advertise through flyers, posters and word of mouth, but using the digital technology available is just smarter and faster.

You have your first customer – now what?

Show up prepared. The best thing you can do, whether you find your customers through an app or word of mouth, is to make a great impression and leave with a great review. Showing up on time and well prepared goes a long way towards that.

Some of the things you can have on hand that you might need:

- Water for you and the dogs

- A foldable dog bowl

- Plastic baggies

- A spare leash in case anything breaks

When you're walking someone else's dog, always be sure to pay attention to them and to your environment. Your job is to keep them safe and comfortable, so don't spend the time on your phone or listening to music. Besides, that's a very bad look if any potential customers see you!

18

DOG-SITTING

Much like dog-walking, dog-sitting is a fantastic way to get involved in your local community and make some money doing so. You will need the same skills and patience you need for walking dogs, but also an appropriate space and much more time. You can find customers in the same way as you would find dog-walking customers: either through traditional publicity or through dedicated apps and websites.

There are two kinds of dog-sitting. The first is where you go over to people's houses and spend time with their dog there. The second is where the dogs come to spend time at your house. Decide which of these services you want to offer or if you can offer both, and start planning your new business.

A local licensing office should be able to help you get the right license to make your business official. Once you've done that, you can start advertising and looking for customers.

What do you need for dog-sitting?

If you want to go to client's houses, you need a car and a very flexible schedule. You will be spending a lot of time at someone else's house, so don't expect to get anything else done in the meantime.

If you are boarding dogs at your house, you will need to have a good, dog-safe space in which to keep them. If you are boarding multiple dogs or have a dog of your own, be prepared that they might just not get along and you will have to keep them separated. Don't assume they can spend time in the same space and never leave dogs together unsupervised, even if they are getting along.

If you are boarding dogs over long periods, they will need to have space where it's safe to leave them unsupervised every now and then. Setting up a space at your house should ideally happen in a separate, empty room which is easy to clean and where you can set up the kinds of things dogs will need: doggie beds, water bowls, chew toys and stuffed toys, etc.

Most clients will give you everything you could possibly need for their dog, but it's always a good idea to have spares and backups. Things like crates and carriers are a must-have, otherwise, you'll be in trouble in case there's an emergency and you need to transport the dog somewhere. Extra toys, chewable treats and leashes are always a good idea.

Before sitting

1. Learn all you can about the dogs that you'll be spending time with. Find out what kind of behavioral problems they have if any, what they're scared of and what they enjoy most.

2. Write down their schedule in detail. The closer you can stick to their schedule, the easier it will be for them. Make a note of feeding times and any medication, as well.

3. Create a list for your client of all the things you will need while dog-sitting. Include their dog's food and medication, bowls, bed, leash and collar, paperwork and a favorite toy.

4. Double-check that you are in agreement on the times, dates, and prices. It's always better to be sure than to discover there was a misunderstanding when the dog is already at your house.

Things to watch out for

1. Be prepared that however well-behaved you were told a dog would be, he will be a little less well-behaved than that.

2. Be prepared that dogs are stressed out when they're moved and their rituals are changed. Try to keep them as comfortable as possible.

3. Be prepared that even potty-trained dogs may have accidents when they're in a new environment. Keep a lot of enzyme cleaner and paper towels on hand, you will need them.

4. Be prepared that looking after multiple dogs is a full-time job and you won't do much else in the meantime.

5. Be prepared for emergencies – have a 24hr clinic phone number on hand, then have a backup clinic too. Make sure you have all the contact information for your clients and then have a backup contact as well.

After sitting

1. Make sure that you return all of the dog's items in good

condition, clean the bowls and make a note of anything that was broken or used up.

2. Give your client a good summary of everything you did, how it went, and whether you had any trouble.

3. Warn your client that their dog might be extra tired or extra active over the next day or two. Any change is stressful and they often react in different ways.

4. Remind your client to give you a good review on your app, website, or to recommend you to their friends! Marketing is always important after a job well done.

ENJOYED THE BOOK?

It really helps out self-publishers like Ashley if you spread the word! If you've learned anything and think the information could be helpful to someone else, please leave a review on Amazon so others in the community can easily find this book!

Made in the USA
Columbia, SC
18 March 2021